Mar...
Reflections in the gr...

21 Ways

Women in Management

Shoot Themselves in the Foot

From the BusinessSuccessCoach.net Series *Reflections in the Glass Ceiling*
© Copyright 2006, John M. McKee, BusinessSuccessCoach.net,
Four Windows - No Walls Consulting, LLC
2456 Oakridge Road • Denver, Colorado • 80135 • USA
All Rights Reserved

Published by Wheatmark®
610 East Delano Street, Suite 104
Tucson, Arizona 85705 U.S.A.
http://www.wheatmark.com

ISBN: 1-58736-618-5
LCCN: 2006922224

Email: John@BusinessSuccessCoach.net
http://www.BusinessSuccessCoach.net

About John McKee & BusinessSuccessCoach.net

As a certified executive coach with nearly thirty years' experience in executive suites and boardrooms across North America, John McKee has amassed unique insights and expert skills to deal with the challenges and opportunities facing executives today. His consultancy, BusinessSuccessCoach.net, reflects his desire to share what he has observed, learned, and practiced during

his professional tenure in organizations ranging from small start-ups to billion-dollar national corporations with thousands of employees.

Over the course of three decades, John has worked in both strongly female- and male-dominated industries and has been responsible for staffing and managing start-ups; hiring, firing, and promoting employees; and overseeing countless layoffs. This broad firsthand experience, coupled with his interest in helping people succeed, is what makes John such a brilliant and inspirational executive coach.

To learn more about John McKee and BusinessSuccessCoach.net, please visit us at http://www.BusinessWomanWeb.com or http://www.BusinessSuccessCoach.net.

What Others Are Saying about John McKee

"John McKee is one of those rare individuals with the right mix of well-defined business acumen and human skills. He is forward thinking and often causes other successful executives to reconsider their entrenched approaches and opinions."

W. A. (Bill) Casamo, Former President, DIRECTV

"John played a significant role in launching our new company from a concept to an operating business in a very short period of time. His extensive knowledge, work ethic, leadership, and substantive participation in strategic meetings all played an important role in the successful launch. He's an all-'round team player with high energy levels—I really enjoyed having him on my team."

Michael S. Alpert, Vice Chairman, Rainbow Media LLC

"Grace, style, witty humor, and amazing insight into the workings of the executive world and human interrelations, John McKee has it all. John has that rare communication style that creates immediate comfort, a strong team dynamic, and an openness to receive new information and explore uncharted territory. Every interaction with John leaves me feeling empowered, enlightened, and capable of amazing feats. Thank you, John!"

Laurie Hayes, Life and Business Coach

"John's style, knowledge, and training were extremely helpful in the development of a new business plan which took us to higher levels than expected or anticipated."

T. R. French, President, French and Company

"John has a no-nonsense approach. He quickly helped me take the actions I needed to get to the next level. I am certain his skills and vast personal experience will help anyone in business . . ."

Randy Otto, President, Automotive Specialty Group

"Executive coaching can be confused with executive therapy. John McKee produces dynamic results with long-term behavior modifications that guarantee success."

Jon Rees, Senior Director, broadcasting industry

"Working with John allows me to entirely change the way I view myself and the people I interact with daily. I never believed I needed coaching—but working with John has accelerated my professional growth tremendously."

Susie Tomenchok, Director, Comcast Media Corporation

"John's depth of knowledge and perspective in business is why I started working with him over ten years ago. His ability to stay focused, bring people together, and make things happen is why I will continue."

T. C. Hunt, Chairman and Cofounder, INSTALLS, Inc.

"The ... careers of those I place through the temporary employment agency that I manage would vastly benefit by the advice imparted in McKee's book. His frank, un-sugarcoated perspective is a wake-up call to working women, and his real-world advice will serve female professionals well in their quest to maximize their career—and thus income-earning—potential.

Robin Gibbons, San Diego Area Manager,
AppleOne Employment Services

TABLE OF CONTENTS

A Message from the Author

Why is a man writing a book designed to help women become more successful at work? I've been asked this question many times over the past few months and it's a great question. My answer: **the sisterhood needs more help from its brothers.**

It's my belief that many men have no idea how difficult it is for women in the workplace, and until men in positions of power start helping them advance into leadership roles, it's going to remain far too hard (unreasonably hard) for women to advance at the rate they deserve. Although legislation and regulatory changes over the '90s were enacted to ensure greater equality in hiring and promotional decisions, I think most business environments are much friendlier to male employees. As a senior executive, I saw how decisions were made when women weren't around. I heard how men discussed their female colleagues in their absence.

I started in business with a female boss, and she set the groundwork for my management development and skills training. During the course of my career, I worked with and for both men and women, in female-dominated industries like cosmetics, fragrances, women's footwear, and jewelry, as well as male-dominated industries like furniture, cable broadcasting, and heavy appliances.

At the jobs I held in female-dominated industries, I was often one of the few men in meetings or travel groups, and I became kind of like "one of the girls." In our after-hours dinners or daily reviews, I learned just how differently women saw things than their male counterparts. They also talked about how tough it was for them compared to guys in similar situations. I was fortunate to have the opportunity to see firsthand how many things a man takes for granted that his female colleagues cannot.

I have been lucky enough to work with a lot of brilliant and talented women. Many of them became my friends. From them I discovered a great deal about different management styles, differences in negotiating, and differences in attitudes. I think male executives could learn a lot from women about building better, more successful organizations if we'd just shut up and listen better. I have also seen many women fail in their professional lives, however, because they simply didn't understand the rules and responsibilities needed to succeed in their chosen professions.

If I've chosen to break ranks, so to speak, with other men, it's entirely because helping women achieve positions of leadership will benefit everyone concerned—women, men, businesses, and society. I hope many men will read this book as well. With new knowledge about issues facing women, they may become more inclined to help their sisters get ahead. More success breeds more success all around—a *circle of success* for all.

One of the problems with writing about women in the workplace is that simply singling women out in any way perpetuates the view that they are different. And while women and men *are* different in many ways, equal opportunity is based on the shared premise that all human beings, regardless of gender, should have the same chance to achieve the goals they set for themselves.

So, to help women succeed in the workplace, and to let you in on the way men think, I've decided to share my insights on the challenges and opportunities facing executives today. It is a reflection of my desire to bring greater understanding and equal opportunity a little bit closer to fruition.

John

Dedications

First and foremost, a huge thank-you to my beautiful wife, Susan McKee. She's been my lover, my partner, and my best friend for over thirty-five years. A woman of unbelievable intuition and generosity, she is—and always has been—the love of my life and my impetus for growth. Without her love, support, humor, challenges, recommendations, and continued life lessons, I would not be the man I am.

Second, to my awesome daughter, Jessica. I hope that in some way this book makes life in the business world better for her and all the women of her generation. Not all the ideas in this book are new, but this may be the first time they've encountered them.

And to Lee Rae McKee.

Acknowledgments

The following individuals had a hand in the creation of this report. Whether directly or through example, each made a valuable contribution.

The Women
Carley Agnew, Roxanne Austin, Stephanie Campbell, Joanne Citro, Susan Collins, Shirley Dawe, Jan Dyamond, Terry Ferguson, Elizabeth Gogel, Cate Hartenstein, Melinda Keith, Helen Latimer, Yolanda Macias, Catherine MacKenzie, Julia McGrath, Susan Mellis, Lisa Peterson, Inga Shelton, Florence Skakum-Lewis, Susan Thompson, Katy Uhl, Kathy Winters

The Men
Barry Agnew, Jay Aldrich, Mickey Alpert, Dr. Alan Banack, Ken Byers, Bill Casamo, Al Guglielmin, Chris Habers, Eddy Hartenstein, Jerry Jellison, Keith McConnell, Randy Otto, Laurie Peet, Jim Ramo, Joel Rochon

Legal Notes

This management report is designed to provide information on how women can increase their chances of succeeding in their careers. It is sold with the understanding that the publisher and author are not engaged in rendering legal, accounting, or other professional services. If legal or other assistance is required, the services of a competent professional should be sought.

It is not the purpose of this report to reprint all the information that is otherwise available to women seeking career advancement, but instead to complement, amplify, and supplement other texts. You are urged to read all available material, learn as much as possible about career advancement, and tailor the information to your individual needs. For more information, see the many resources listed in our appendix.

Every effort has been made to make this report as complete and as accurate as possible. However, there may be mistakes, both typographical and in content. Therefore, this text should be used only as a general guide and not as the ultimate source of advice to women on how to succeed in the corporate world. Furthermore, this book contains information that is current up to the printing date.

The purpose of this report is to educate and entertain. As with any advice, it is strongly recommended that the reader use his or her own judgment when determining the appropriateness of the advice for his or her particular situation. The author and publisher shall have neither liability nor responsibility to any person or entity with respect to any loss or damage caused, or alleged to have been caused, directly or indirectly, by the information contained in this book.

If you do not wish to be bound by the above, you may return this book for a full refund.

Limits of Liability / Disclaimer of Warranty

The authors and publisher of this book and the accompanying materials have put forth their best efforts in preparing this program.

The authors and publisher make no representation or warranties with respect to the accuracy, applicability, fitness, or completeness of the contents of this program.

They disclaim any warranties (expressed or implied), merchantability, or fitness for any particular purpose.

The authors and publisher shall in no event be held liable for any loss or other damages, including but not limited to special, incidental, consequential, or other damages.

As always, the advice of a competent legal, tax, accounting, or other professional should be sought. The authors and publisher do not warrant the performance, effectiveness, or applicability of any sites listed in this book. All links are for informational purposes only and are not warranted for content, accuracy, or any other implied or explicit purpose.

This book contains material protected under International and Federal Copyright Laws and Treaties.

Any unauthorized use of this material is prohibited.

Microsoft, Microsoft Outlook, and related names are the property of Microsoft Corporation.

21 Ways

Women in Management

Shoot Themselves in the Foot

Chapter 1

WANTING TO HAVE IT ALL

"I've yet to be on a campus where most women weren't worrying about some aspect of combining marriage, children, and a career. I've yet to find one where many men were worrying about the same thing."

Gloria Steinem

Perhaps you've heard some of these recommendations before:

- Always be true to yourself

- Maintain your essence in all situations

- Balance your family and your career

I personally believe these are well-conceived and well-intended ideas. As a human being, a business coach, and a former executive in corporate America I couldn't argue with anyone who offers these excellent pieces of advice. Quite simply, a woman should be able to have a successful career while at the same time enjoying her personal life.

But I haven't met a lot of women who've succeeded in doing so. It's really tough to maintain the balance needed for a healthy personal life while working in an environment that may be competitive internally and externally. And unfortunately, there simply is no silver bullet one can keep in a magical revolver and use to stop every problem in its tracks. The same can be said for men to some extent; but in my opinion, these issues are far more important and have greater ramifications for women.

Men are prone to accept the maxim that "behind every great career is a broken marriage," and the trophy wife (who is younger and prettier than a former partner) remains a status symbol that accompanies the expensive car, the title, and the grand home. It's part of the package. I find women to be a lot deeper than most guys. They, more often than not, really want to be able to balance each of the three key elements in their lives—their careers, their families, and their essence.

For nearly thirty years, I've seen female friends and colleagues suffer as they tried to be superwomen who could do it all. And while men have faced similar issues more frequently in the past five years, it remains primarily a female concern. Most women still want it all, and this can put them at a competitive disadvantage with their male colleagues.

If you want to reach the top, you must decide that you are prepared to do what it takes to get ahead—even if that means "giving at the office" at the expense of your home life and yourself. Not everyone desires entry into the most senior ranks of corporate America, but if it is your dream to break the glass ceiling, then you need to put your career first. That's what the guys are doing. This isn't to say I'm a proponent of any approach that dictates *career at any cost.* In fact, most of my work with clients of either gender focuses more on having a successful life on all fronts, not just work. The key is to know what you want and understand what is required to achieve it.

Tips on How to Use This Management Report

- Decide just how dedicated you are to getting ahead in your career. Are you prepared to do what it takes to achieve recognition or beat others out for that promotion?

- Recognize that when it comes to competing with men, you are usually at a disadvantage. Because of your gender you will tend to be more holistic in outlook and more caring toward others than men.

- Use what works for you in your situation at this time in your career and life. And throw away the rest of this book.

- Don't accept any advice without testing it yourself first.

Chapter 2

NOT HAVING A PERSONAL LIFE PLAN

"We tend to get what we expect."

Norman Vincent Peale
Methodist Episcopal minister
and author

I have had the privilege of spending time with many well-known and well-regarded company and political leaders. I have met and worked with people like the chairmen and CEOs of such organizations as DIRECTV, General Motors, The Hudson's Bay Company, AT&T, and Cablevision. I met and worked with former federal government secretaries and, in Canada, cabinet ministers. I was invited to breakfast with former president Bill Clinton. Being up close and personal with these individuals caused me to realize, at some stage in my executive life, that most of them share certain attributes. I started to ask people I regarded as very successful to tell me one or two things they'd picked up that they attributed to their current status in life.

I found that virtually all of them had a personal life plan. Almost to a person, they could tell me what the future was going to be like for them. Their plan wasn't always written down, but it was always fairly detailed, including deadlines and clear goals. In short, a business plan for their career and life.

Now compare that to most people in the world. Most people are not as happy as they would like to be, as successful as they think they should be, or as wealthy as they'd hoped they'd be when they were younger. Not coincidently, most people do not have a personal life plan either. They simply get up each day, do whatever it is that they get paid to do, and then do whatever it is they think they want to do in their leisure time.

In short, they let life happen to them as opposed to managing their lives.

In my coaching business, I have found that personal life planning and management is something almost no women in management practice. I don't know why. But I regard the neglect of this activity to be one of the single most critical mistakes they make. For the most part, these women wouldn't dream of trying to run their business or department without a plan detailed by activities, expected outcomes, and time frames.

But they overlook managing their lives in a similar fashion. This is just plain goofy. If you want something, you should have a plan as to how you will get it. And, in general, the more detailed your plan is, the more likely you will achieve it.

A good life plan must recognize that our lives are divided into three different kinds of activities and elements. Each of us is:

- A professional—the one who goes out each day to make a living. This part of us is focused on our paycheck and status, where we work, and the company or industry in which we work.

- A personal being—the one who does things for and with those we love. This part of us is replenished by the things we love and activities we enjoy.

- A financial manager—the one who tries to ensure we have the resources to do what we want and get what we want, now and in the future.

Having a good life plan is even more critical for a woman than it is for a man. By the time they enter the workplace, women tend to care more about others' well being than men do. It's easier for women to fail to look after themselves because they are more preoccupied with helping others in their lives. If you want to get ahead in business, your life plan needs to address how those you care for will be looked after. Not having the appropriate support network—be it a house-keeper, gardener, or nanny—will hinder your success.

Creating a life plan is work. Developing it will be as hard as one allows it to become. Some of my female clients have created detailed, viable multi-year plans in just a couple of hours. Afterward, these individuals enjoyed amazing success in a very short period of time. Other clients have labored over the concept and never really completed a plan they could act upon. Those individuals continued to experience many of the same issues and roadblocks for a long time.

The more detailed your life plan, the more readily you can identify areas of weakness and find ways to overcome them. If you need experience in a branch office to get a promotion, for instance, you can begin negotiating for such a position.

Like insurance, you should review your plan after any major life event. Getting married, or divorced, starting a family, moving, a pro-motion, illness, any of these things can render your life plan obsolete. Since a life plan is one of the most important tools you have for achieving your goals, make sure it's current. Don't treat it as a static document; it's much too critical to be relegated to the bottom drawer.

I had a client, "Karen," who was a successful executive in a large telecommunications corporation. She was generally happy with her career and was making a decent income. On the home front, she had a partner and three children and loved them all. She was in better-than-average shape physically, and was psychologically healthy as well. She created her plan in very little time and had little doubt that taking control of her life on each front would pay off for her. Less than six months after developing her personal life plan:

- She was promoted (part of her plan for "within one year"), and nearly doubled her income (also part of her plan for "within one year").

- She had discussed issues with her partner, her kids, and her parents that had been troubling her for a long time. Consequently, each relationship is doing far better than it had been (part of her plan for "within two years").

- She began to take more time for personal and creative activities, which contributed to a greater sense of serenity and well-being (part of her plan for "immediate and ongoing life management").

- She rented a second home for getaways (part of her plan for "in three years").

Needless to say, Karen believes in life plans. To learn more about creating one for yourself, see pages 103–116.

Tips for a Successful Personal Life Plan

- Your first task is to decide what you want your life to look like in the future. Consider everything, not just a few obvious issues facing you today. Include items like fitness, relationships, time for yourself, your family, possessions, spiritual or religious choices, and mental health.

- Many people only focus on short-term goals regarding money, career, or relationships because they think that's what will make their life satisfying. Concentrating solely on the things that bring instant gratification, however, will often lead to dissatisfaction or unhappiness elsewhere.

- Remember that many individuals appear successful, yet aren't happy or satisfied because they don't take the time to look at their situation holistically.

- Once you've decided what your life would look like in an ideal world, make some decisions about when each of your goals should be realized. Be realistic, but don't be afraid to push yourself either.

- Statistics show that 86 percent of those who complete and use a life plan report that they are happier and more satisfied with their situations than those who do not. It may take time, but you will get real benefits.

- See the appendix on page 103 for more details and specific guidelines.

Chapter 3

TOLERATING GENDER BIAS

"We still think of a powerful man as a born leader and a powerful woman as an anomaly."

Margaret Atwood
Journalist and author

Unacceptable fact: Less than 4 percent of America's largest corporations are run by female CEOs. This despite statistics indicating that women are graduating in higher numbers than men, and that women are starting more new businesses than men. So, maybe there's more than rude comments and bad attitudes at play here. If gender bias isn't a factor, then why aren't more women holding top leadership positions in America's corporations?

You'd think in this day and age that sexism in the workplace would be nonexistent, wouldn't you? In fact, conditions have improved, and my younger clients and colleagues often say they've never experienced it. However, it is still out there, affecting work performance, opportunities for advancement, and job satisfaction for many women.

And here's the thing: It's going to remain an issue until women stop being "understanding" of men who are gender biased. I realize it's natural for many individuals to try to see the best in others. That's a great thing and helps to offset the Moaning Minnies of the world who only see the worst in us. But as long as so many women continue to accept others' personal biases, it's going to be tougher for a lot of deserving women to get ahead.

When men are sexist, or even just out of touch with what's right, it is not good for any person or business. It's particularly bad for the woman who is trying to get ahead today, and for the next generation of female managers.

I hear ladies saying that they can accept men's sexism because the guys "don't know any better," or "don't mean anything negative" by their comments or actions, that they are "good-hearted people." These individuals will point out all the good things done by men who seem to believe they are still living in the late 1950s, when the business world was dominated by other (mostly white) men. And what they say may well be true. Perhaps these throwbacks really have made solid contributions to the world around them. But we can applaud those actions while still expecting more.

All other things being equal, the law of averages would suggest that more women should be in leadership positions. But they aren't, and that's simply not acceptable. America's corporations are full of bored, unproductive employees, and our position in the global marketplace is getting worse each year. We need some new ideas, new approaches, and new leadership. It's time we had more women in the highest echelons of our society. Meg Whitman of eBay and a few other female CEOs can't carry the ball by themselves.

The injustice of keeping qualified women out of the top jobs aside, corporate America is hurting itself, and hurting our competitiveness in the ever-expanding global marketplace. So if you think that gender bias isn't a real problem, you may want to reconsider your stance. Even as this book was going to press, Neil French, head of WPP Group, one of the world's largest advertising agencies, made headlines by stating that there would never be as many women in senior man-agement because they prefer to have babies.

Tips for Dealing with Gender Bias

- First and foremost, believe in yourself as a professional. Stand tall, focus on your goals, and try to keep productivity high.

- Don't volunteer to do any task that might underscore sexist perceptions (like ordering lunch for coworkers).

- Actively demonstrate behavior that contradicts stereotypes. If you're able to travel, for instance, say so. If you're comfortable with taking risks, look for ways to indicate this.

- Find inspiration from the Civil Rights era. Tolerance for bad behavior was set aside in order to promote a better, more equitable way. Change did not come easily; it took time and perseverance.

- See if there is an opportunity to work with your company's human resources department to organize a seminar or workshop to help improve relations.

- There is no point in suffering the effects of bias. Unless you are proactive, the problem will not go away.

Chapter 4

MISUNDERSTANDING THE BUSINESS CIRCLE OF SUCCESS

"A little more matriarchy is what the world needs, and I know it. Period. Paragraph."

Dorothy Thompson
Journalist and author

A common piece of advice for managers is that they should spend a great deal of time getting to know their staff. Work side-by-side to ensure that each employee knows what he or she needs to do. While that idea is well intentioned, it's never going to provide maximum benefit—to anyone involved.

Smart businesswomen recognize that their bosses are often so busy getting their own jobs done, they may not notice that those underneath them are in need of more time, attention, or resources. So here's a tip that you won't read in the management texts out there:

It is more important that you, the manager, spend time helping your boss look good. And you need to do this at every opportunity. When the boss understands that you are able to help him or her succeed, you and your team will get more time, attention, and resources. With the tools you need to improve effectiveness and productivity, your team will become more successful. Your team's enhanced productivity will lead your boss to see you as a more effective manager. (S)he will again give you more of the resources you need, making you even more effective. Your heightened productivity will reflect well on her or him. This is the circle of success.

Making the boss look good is similar to properly promoting yourself, but for many women, easier to implement. Now your ability to see things from someone else's perspective pays off. It's really not that different from a concept we're all familiar with: excellent customer service. Just think of your boss as your customer.

Keep your boss informed of results and key developments in your area of responsibility. Prior to the boss's monthly meeting with his or her superior, try to anticipate areas of concern and prepare him or her to deal with potential questions. Meet your performance objectives. Watch your boss's back and don't speak ill of him or her in meetings.

Your performance will affect how others in the company perceive your boss's effectiveness. Make sure you and your staff are always prepared for meetings, and behave in a professional manner. Don't allow problems to surprise your boss. Keep him or her informed about what you're hearing on the grapevine; it's not always idle gossip.

Making the boss look good is not to be confused with being a yes-woman. It's not at all the same thing. Standing up to the boss and preventing him or her from making the wrong decision is good business. Just use common sense and be aware of when and where to deliver this type of message.

Results equal rewards

Companies spend a lot of money developing and implementing new systems to help automate and, we hope, increase the efficiency of the whole company. After these significant investments, managers are told to become system experts to ensure all the intended benefits are realized. Such expectations often create an environment where you begin to feel your most important task is to learn the ins and outs of the system. You couldn't be more wrong.

Efficiency (knowing how to make the systems perform better) is not the same as *effectiveness* (improving results)—and effectiveness is what will make you and your boss look good. Your department has certain objectives against which your performance and career potential will be measured. By focusing on becoming a system expert, you take your eye off the ball and risk not meeting those objectives. Don't get distracted.

Tips for Working the Circle of Success

- Keep close to your boss—know her and how she operates.

- Make certain your boss knows how you operate. Give the boss all the knowledge he needs to help promote or bonus you to the highest levels.

- Remember this Japanese management maxim: "I don't like that man, so I must spend more time with him." The information in this chapter is particularly important if you don't like your boss, or she doesn't like you.

Chapter 5

NOT SEPARATING THE PERSONAL FROM THE PROFESSIONAL

"It is impossible for your body to live separate and apart from the journey of your spirit."

Caroline Myss
Author

What happens in the workplace often takes on a more personal meaning for women than it does for the hairier sex.

For many reasons, men can more easily separate their work from their inner selves. I've had many male clients tell me that they think of themselves as baseball players who do the best they can for whoever is paying them at the time. They often view their current workplace as a stopover on the way to another job and consequently are less likely to have any personal relationships with people of either sex at the office. That's part of the reason why it's hard for some women to understand the concept, "It's just business and not personal."

Women are far more likely to take things to heart. While that's a great attribute in many other facets of life, it can handicap their growth in a business environment. I believe many female managers have suffered career slowdown or even derailment because they took a comment or review more personally than would their male counterparts.

Just because someone was tough on you, don't assume that you've been singled out. And if you've had a bad review, or the boss has just told you that you really blew it, don't think your career progess has come full stop. It usually doesn't mean that at all. In this particular instance you didn't perform as expected or hoped, and that's it. When the review is over, simply dust yourself off and get on with life. Very likely the heated statements were nothing that anyone will remember for a long time. The comments were "just business."

This tendency to react to the personal elements of a situation can take another, insidious form. I have seen many women in management change their behavior when they think someone (usually a supervisor or boss) is attracted to them. They might dress in a more feminine manner (skirts instead of suits), speak in a higher-pitched voice, or otherwise act more "girly." This hurts them in several ways: They may not compare favorably when the next promotional decision arises because the boss wants someone more tough and street smart. They may damage their relationships with their peers because they look like they're sucking up. They may appear willing to go up the ladder on their backs, which turns their female colleagues off and limits how much help they will offer.

As an example, one of my clients, "Janice," was an attractive, tall, intelligent woman who had learned very young that she could use her features and sensuality to get many of the things she wanted. Now in an executive role, she noticed that her chief operating officer was paying a lot of attention to her, and thought she might be getting a promotion soon. After all, he often had meetings with her—without her boss in attendance—and in those meetings he discussed other people in their corporation and shared his opinions about them.

Though he made it obvious that he was attracted to her, Janice thought he was primarily interested in her career development. Turned out he was just a guy who liked to be around good-looking women.

Don't think that because he's showing an attraction to you, you are special. This kind of attention is still just part of the business world—a nastier part that you should steer clear of whenever possible.

Tips for Keeping Yourself from Taking Things Too Personally

- Develop a thicker skin, or at least a sheath, that will help you deflect any comments or looks that would ordinarily inflict a psychological wound. And take the time to think about what is transpiring so you can rationally determine how you want to deal with it—whether to ignore it and move on, discuss it, or make a countermove.

- Try imagining how a male colleague would react if he were in your shoes. Chances are you won't picture him licking his wounds. He's already moved on.

- Remind yourself that this is a business. Focus on the business at hand: solving problems, developing programs, increasing sales—whatever it is that you're there to do.

- Keep in mind there's a reason why many of the nation's business leaders are called old boys—they still think the same way about women as guys half their ages! Ignore any unprofessional attention you might receive and respond in a professional manner.

- To quote Richard Carlson, "Don't sweat the small stuff … and it's all small stuff."

Chapter 6

THINKING WE BOTH SPEAK THE SAME LANGUAGE

"The purpose of learning is growth, and our minds, unlike our bodies, can continue growing as we continue to live."

Mortimer J. Adler
Educator and philosopher

"Why is it that when I tell a man 'no,' they don't get it? I mean what is it about the word that they don't understand? Are they so totally driven by their hormones that they lose their hearing?"

There's something I'd guess most readers have heard or said more than once.

It's a great example for this chapter because it shows just how differently women and men can hear the same thing. That difference has a huge impact on women's success in the business world.

Many of you will no doubt remember the book *Men Are from Mars, Women Are from Venus* by John Gray. Although much of what it brought into general awareness is considered common knowledge today, it was a big deal when first released. And although the book deals with romantic relationships, his main premise—how different the sexes are when it comes to communication—holds true for the office as well as the bedroom.

The communication issue is an old one, of course. I suspect it's existed since men and women first started sharing the work of skinning the mammoths for dinner. Of all the issues I work on with my clients, the seond most important involves how we communicate with each other differently, and what we really mean when we say something.

Since the workplace was first a male stronghold, it has, over time, developed a masculine culture. As women have worked their way up the corporate ladder, that culture has started to evolve. But evolution takes time, with members of each gender struggling to understand and accommodate the other.

Different characteristics show themselves to different degrees in different arenas. I may have communication skills that are stereotypically feminine, or you may have a competitive streak that people consider masculine. And, there's a lot of research indicating that age makes a difference here. Those who were raised in the '80s have a very different set of experiences, and view of the world, than children of the '60s.

If you grew up on Madonna you are likely to be less content with being put in a box than those women who grew up on ABBA or even the B-52s. To state the obvious, sometimes women in their late twenties feel more kinship with young men than they do with women in their forties. What we are dealing with here is not simply a gender issue, but a complex web of human relations in which workers try to gain respect, demonstrate accomplishment, and, we hope, move up the ranks.

Each of us has attributes that are considered to be more prevalent in either women or men. And these attributes can either work for or against us as we strive to build our careers. Being aware of these differences can be invaluable when it comes to interpreting the words and actions of those around us. Understanding what our behavior communicates to those who control our future is vital.

Although it's dangerous to generalize to the degree I am about to … here goes. Following are a few examples of characteristics that differentiate the sexes. They are not my ideas alone, and consequently they have a place in business folklore.

You may have seen or heard some of these in other forms, or from other management types; they are pretty commonsense and often repeated in day-to-day discussions. And again I will tell you, don't trust that any of these are always right and true. Test them yourself.

Friendship

- Women see friendship more as a matter of connection. They don't tie it to place or time.

- Men tend to be friendlier initially, but they also come and go more readily. They see their loyalty as being first to the team/employer.

Communication

- Women wait their turn to talk. *Then they talk to think.*

- Men interrupt. *They think to talk.*

This means women will work through the issue aloud while men will be silent while they work it through, then give the answer and explain how they got there.

Organizational Preference

- Women prefer a flat organizational structure. They are more inclined to share power and decision making, i.e, teamsmanship.

- Men prefer a hierarchy with a clear definition of power. They like sports that way and they like business charts that way. Especially when they have the best title!

Process vs. Outcome

- Women are process-oriented—see "Communication." The downside to this in a group environment is that they may frustrate the guys who don't understand that they are processing aloud.

- Men are goal-oriented. As above. They like to say, "Here's the answer and here's how we get to it." Women should adopt this style in mixed-sex meetings, especially if the boss is male—it's the approach of choice in a business environment.

Games

- Women play with those they like, and identify themselves with where they work and what they do.

- Men play with those who will win, and see their employer as just an employer, not an identifier of who they are.

Conflict Management

- Women avoid conflict. I know this one is probably the most likely to get a reaction from readers—especially those under thirty-five or so. Tip: If you are dealing with someone who avoids conflict, try to work with her or him in a win/win manner so they will be less closed.

- Men deal with conflict—at least at work. Ironically, they are not nearly as good at this when it comes to personal issues.

Negotiation

- Women take the word "no" at face value.

- Men don't.

For reasons that have more to do with nurture than nature, words just don't mean the same thing to men and women. Children are born negotiators. Most children have direct experience turning "no" into "yes." Somewhere along the way, though, girls seem to lose this ability, or they feel uncomfortable exercising it at work. For a boy, these early experiences combined with sports experience, where negotiating for playing time is common, means he enters the work-force having learned that when you hear the word no, it really means "Convince me." When he's with a young woman who says the no-word again, do you see how he might behave because of how he experiences that word?

Until the most recent generation entered the workforce, only a very small percentage of women had been raised playing competitive games or sports as youngsters. For many women, games had a lot to do with every player having fun and feeling like they'd all played equally well.

Later on in his life, when he's on the job, and a supervisor or boss tells him his work is not that good, and he'd better pick up the pace or he's out of there, the guy just focuses on the first part of the message—pick up the pace. But when his female counterpart hears that feedback, she may take it to mean something entirely different.

A woman's focus on process may lead her to hear the comment that ended with "or you're out of here" to mean that she's not going anywhere in the company ever, or even that she's about to be let go.

In other circumstances, imagine the woman who has done good work and wants to discuss her promotion opportunities with a male supervisor. If she's told no, you can see how she might take that no and move on to something else, leaving the man to wonder why she didn't even try to persuade him. In his mind, her lack of follow-through may have actually hurt her chances for a promotion. In her mind, he's just shutting her down.

With such different styles and assumptions, misunderstandings are commonplace, and opportunities for both gaining understanding and working together effectively are lost.

Two More Tips for Cracking the Language Barrier

- To counteract communication differences, ask questions to clarify what has been said. When told no, ask if additional information might help change his mind. Or, repeat what you think he meant so the guy you are trying to communicate with has an opportunity to clarify or adjust his communication based on your assumptions.

- By using this technique, you are both learning more about each other's style of communication. Learning each other's language is essential to productivity and your job satisfaction.

Chapter 7

AVOIDING SELF-PROMOTION

"The more you praise and celebrate your life, the more there is in life to celebrate."

Oprah Winfrey
TV personality, producer, and author

I want to be really clear about this: *it is entirely to your benefit to ensure that the people in a position to affect your career advancement are aware of who you are and what you are contributing.*

Most women don't like to boast or brag. Flaunting success or trying to prove something to others is an uncomfortable feeling for most women, even though only they perceive their actions as flaunting. Men like to one-up each other; not so women.

In general, women have a hard time drawing attention to themselves in business situations and corporate environments. When offered a new office with their promotion, they may feel that it's not really necessary—the one they have is good enough. Women are happier letting their work speak for itself.

Over the years, I have observed that women often feel they don't deserve their success. They tend to either sell their accomplishments short or attribute the success to a team effort. Instead of recognizing that their success came from hard work and perseverance, women think they just got lucky.

And to a greater extent than the guys they compete with, women want to be liked, and they feel that a promotion might alienate them from their peers and cause resentment.

Do not think, as too many women are prone to, that the quality of your work will speak for itself. This presumes that bosses have time to investigate what their employees are up to. They don't. Think of it this way: To be promoted, whether male or female, you need to not simply meet your performance objectives, but exceed them. Failing to make decision makers aware of your exceptional performance is not logical. You worked hard to achieve those results—don't let them go unnoticed.

Embracing the art of self-promotion is something women tend not to do. Yet it's a crucial career move for anyone who wants to lay the groundwork for future opportunities. And a lot of the men you are competing with are very skilled at it.

There are many reasons why most women shy away from self-promotion. In general, it boils down to this: they don't want to appear too pushy or money-hungry because they have more class than guys, and because they've been socialized to act reserved and polite.

I used to believe that this would become less of an issue when more women were running organizations, but I've since learned that female managers can just as readily miss their bright, talented junior managers' contributions. So it's incumbent on the individual to go out of her way to ensure that her successes are recognized. I don't recommend bragging, but there are other ways of calling attention to your work.

You can help your boss and your company if you let them know more about you. I consider this a big part of managing your career.

It's work, and like all work it can be a bit uncomfortable or difficult. But the other option is just hoping that others notice you and give you a break. And I have never been a fan of any management activity that is based upon hope and crossed fingers.

A few common mistakes:

- Not making small talk with the boss.

In many organizations, the only time we come face-to-face with the boss is in the hallway or elevator. Give your boss a break and help him or her know who you are and what you're working on. A simple comment about a task you performed successfully may make you more memorable to someone who will decide who to promote in the future. If that's too much, just talking about your interests outside of work may be useful. Glance at the headlines in the sports section of your newspaper before coming to work and keep abreast of current events; you'll never be at a loss for something to say.

I've made a lot of decisions about whom to promote in my career, and I can assure you that the people I knew best were the first ones who came to mind. Regardless of what the human resources team told me about the candidates' performance reviews, I often based my choices on what I knew about the individuals I was most familiar with.

- Thinking your good work will speak for itself.

It might, but why take chances? If you don't speak up, credit for your work may go to someone else without your knowing it.

- Not going out for drinks after work to review the day and learn from it.

This one's a biggie. The opportunity to sit with a supervisor or boss should not be passed up. It gives you a chance to show her or him more about you than you can in a dozen formal meetings. Attend company-sponsored events (like picnics and holiday parties), conferences, and seminars. Don't arrive late or leave early. Make sure you pay your respects to the most senior company representative in attendance.

- Assuming the person above you will properly attribute credit to you—and not steal it.

Don't overlook the importance of promoting your accomplishments with others within your industry. One easy way to keep your name on the top of the pile is to send along interesting clippings or news items to members of your network.

- Sharing credit with others more frequently than men do.

As a society I wish we did more of this. It builds stronger teams and ultimately better success. But as your business success coach, I will tell you to be mindful about how much credit you give away. Someone who doesn't know you well enough may believe that you didn't do as much as you did.

In general, you have to realize that simply completing your tasks, no matter how competently or efficiently, is not enough to get you further along in your career path. You could end up continuing in your present position for a long time.

Why?

Because performing effectively is quite different than being *perceived* as performing effectively. The first will get you ignored, the second will help you achieve your objectives. And being passed up for great assignments, promotions, and raises is certainly not your objective.

It's hard, but vitally important for women to become comfortable with talking about themselves and their accomplishments. Men do quite well at pumping themselves up as assets to the company, so why not you?

Most women tend to think about what's good for the company, without planning their own strategy for advancement. One way to think about self-promotion is to realize that you, your ideas, your energy, your accomplishments, and your deserved advancement are all good for the company.

If the work that you are doing is valuable, if it meets or exceeds its intended purpose, if it achieves its goals, then why shouldn't you be rewarded for your efforts?

Self-promotion is not the same as bragging. Self-promotion is not the same as being arrogant, aloof, annoying, or obnoxious. In fact, self-promotion is nothing more than being honest about a job you've done well and allowing the credit to come to you.

It's all part of the business game, and again, it's an important part. Make it a habit to get the word out and you'll definitely see an upward spiral in your career.

Tips on Self-Promotion

- Complete your life plan and include a vision for your self-promotion. Develop a list of all the activities that will showcase your knowledge and make others more aware of your skills and achievements.

- Start observing how others talk about their accomplishments and ideas. Make a mental note of how they deliver the information to others. Also note how their audience reacts. By putting these two activities together you can begin to fashion your own approach.

- Target people in your firm that you should establish a relationship with. Show them you're thinking about things by emailing them relevant press clippings or sending them important information.

- Express your informed opinion at meetings and whenever speaking with colleagues and your boss.

- Volunteer to take on a task or project. Being proactive and enthusiastic are positive traits.

- Join and participate in professional organizations. The more people you can interact with, the more opportunities you'll have to promote yourself.

- When you give talks or take advantage of training and educational opportunities, don't forget to let your boss know.

- If you win an award, let your in-house newsletter know.

Chapter 8

LACKING EXECUTIVE PRESENCE, PART A: HESITATING TO SPEAK UP AND SPEAK STRONG

"Believe in yourself. You gain strength, courage, and confidence by every experience in which you stop to look fear in the face ... You must do that which you think you cannot do."

Eleanor Roosevelt
First lady and member of the UN's
Commission on Human Rights

It's a sad fact of life that many top players in business reach that level not because of proven business acumen, but because they have a combination of elusive qualities that add to up what's called "executive presence." They sound like leaders and look like leaders. Many company boards put far too much stock in this trait when recruiting a new CEO, overlooking smart, skilled, capable individuals who don't exude as much confidence.

Time and again, when I role-play with clients, I see women speaking more tentatively than their male peers. They allow themselves to be interrupted. They defer more to others. In short, they lack executive presence.

If you want to get ahead in today's workplace you need to find your voice. Your voice is your identity, your sense of self, your relationship to others, your sense of purpose. Your voice is the power to express your ideas clearly and concisely, making certain you are recognized for your contributions. Regardless of what you do or where you work, it will play a large role in determining how people relate to you.

An executive's style of communicating significantly influences how she is perceived by others in the organization. How we sound—our pitch, tone, and volume—will affect how well our audience listens.

How can you use your voice to its best advantage?

When you must speak to a group of people, don't underestimate the importance of preparation. Research your subject and put together a presentation complete with appropriate audio-visual aids. Practice, practice, practice. Try to anticipate what kinds of questions you might get and compose some answers in advance. Don't read from your notes.

Before you begin your oration, be aware of any obstacles that might hinder your audience's ability to hear you clearly. Does the air conditioning unit make noise? Will the sound from the projector compete with your voice? Will there be other conversations going on at the same time? Knowing beforehand what you will be up against can greatly enhance your confidence when you are speaking.

As you begin your talk, make eye contact with those around you and project your voice to the group. Even if it's a tough room because the topic is unpleasant, use nonverbal cues to help get people on your side. Smile warmly, but don't overdo it. Make your voice more animated by raising and lowering volume, or adding some inflections. Phrase your statements in a manner that engages as opposed to driving people to daydream. Don't be afraid to look at anyone, and don't give the appearance of being shy or frightened—even if you are! Try to appear relaxed and self-assured.

If you don't feel confident about your public speaking skills, sign up for a course. As a senior executive, you'll find you are speaking in front of groups, either formally or informally, on a regular basis. Don't let poor skills hinder your career advancement.

How about those weekly department or team meetings? First, choose your seat wisely. You want to be visible to the person running things, not out of sight. If you are a new participant, or you have been promoted, or you want to be seen as a mover and shaker, it's a good idea to take a place of importance at the table. That way, when you have something to say, everyone can see and hear you.

Speaking of being seen and heard, women tend not to interrupt or even speak up as frequently as their male counterparts. When they do, it is often with less conviction. This trait may stem from how they were taught to participate in conversations. In many situations, girls and young women learn that being polite (not interrupting others) and reserved (ladylike) is more acceptable.

Go into your meeting well prepared, with perhaps a few speaking points written down. Rehearse some polite ways to interrupt the flow if you expect one or two individuals to dominate the meeting. Say something like, "On that topic, I have a point I would like to make," and then articulate it clearly, making eye contact with those around the table. Sit up straight. Look powerful. If you're interrupted, calmly remind the other speaker that you have not finished making your point and then go on speaking.

In my last role in corporate America, I was with DIRECTV. We held weekly meetings, and as the company grew, the number of people attending grew. Soon there was no longer room for everyone at the table. Although about 40 percent of the attendees were women, only a few sat at the table. Many of the wallflowers were powerful, smart women who acted with great confidence in other environments.

But because of their lack of presence in these meetings, many of the senior executives had no idea how talented they were.

The consequences of not speaking up are dire. Over time, you risk being left out, taken advantage of, and regarded by some as less worthy. In many cases, the guy in the seat across the table will get the credit for a great idea instead of you, while you seem invisible, apologetic. Clearly it hurts your chances for advancement if you are not regarded as good leadership material. And self-confidence is the key for any leader.

Speaking up is not hostile, threatening, or demanding. You are not trespassing on the rights of others. Begin to really believe that speaking up is a positive trait—an honest and appropriate expression of your ideas and needs. And consider the flip side of this. If you don't speak up and get your ideas and convictions across to others, how will they know what you are thinking? How will they understand what you feel or believe if you don't share that with them in a meaningful and powerful way?

If what you have to say is important then it is your responsibility to say it—clearly and with conviction. Wait too long to speak your mind and someone else in the room might communicate your idea before you do, winning the glory.

For the introverts of the world, both male and female, it can be difficult to be heard in a room full of extroverts. Many successful business leaders think quickly on their feet, and those who need more time can be perceived as less bright or less committed to the task. If you're an introvert you'll need to take extra steps to ensure your message isn't getting lost. Preparation for meetings both large and small is essential. If there is no set agenda, try to anticipate potential topics of discussion. And make sure you reward yourself with a little quiet time or a solitary walk after the meeting.

Learning to speak up takes time and practice. When you've done it well, give yourself a good pat on the back. When you've had a setback, just think about how you can better handle the situation next time and move on. Over time, better habits will form and speaking up will become second nature to you. You'll even come to enjoy it.

Tips for Finding Your Voice

- Don't be a wallflower and wait to be asked. If you have an opinion, voice it. If an opportunity to work on an interesting project or committee arises, don't wait for an invitation; let your supervisor know you'd like to work on it.

- Prepare for meetings in advance. Review the agenda, minutes, email correspondence, etc. so you can prepare some notes to help you feel confident.

- Walk into a meeting knowing where you'd like to sit and take that seat—and not the seat in the back where the key players can't see you.

- Don't weaken your argument by overexplaining. When you try to soften your message by explaining it, you lose your audience and undermine your point.

- If you have the floor, don't waste time giving credit to everyone who helped you come up with the point you're making. Again, your audience's attention will wander if you get off message.

- Work with your mentor to improve your confidence in your speaking ability. Set goals.

Chapter 9

LACKING EXECUTIVE PRESENCE, PART B: NOT LOOKING AND ACTING THE PART

"Your vision will become clear only
When you look into your heart.
Who looks outside, dreams;
Who looks inside, awakens."

Carl Jung
Psychoanalyst

Every year, companies around the world spend billions of dollars packaging their products, and for good reason. The package tells an important story about what's inside. It lets people know what the product is made of, how it will benefit them, and who it's for.

Here are five key things you need to know about packaging yourself if you wish to maximize your career potential.

1. You must convey dominance. Regardless of whether you're a woman or a man, your chances of reaching the top are better if you're taller. If you aren't tall, make the most of every inch you have. My experience has taught me that physical presence causes others to take us seriously, both at work and in our personal lives. I have never encountered a successful CEO who failed to make his or her presence known.

The ability to communicate dominance is essential for any leader. Without it you will be overlooked, ignored, and undervalued—not a good position to be in when it's time for a promotion or pay raise.

Executive presence is also communicated through body language. It's only logical to assume that the person who hunches her shoulders or looks at the floor pales in comparison to the one who purposefully strides into the room, giving eye contact, regardless of intelligence and talent. Those who were taught as children to have a high sense of self-worth project their presence loud and clear. For others it is something that, with much concentration, can be learned. Do not focus on building actual self-esteem or confidence. Practices that support the qualities of confidence will yield more immediate results.

You don't have to feel sure of yourself to act sure of yourself. You don't have to be in control to appear in control. Act the part and in time you'll begin to feel the part.

2. "Dress for success" still applies. Rightly or not, society is less critical of slovenly men than slovenly women. I am constantly surprised by how some male professionals look while on the job. They may be paunchy, with their pants hanging off of them because they can't be done up around that large waist; they may have unkempt hair (facial and head); and they may not worry about coordinating clothes with their ties, belts, shoes, or watches—but they still get promoted or achieve success in their fields. Do you think a woman would be as likely identified as a promotable manager if she had a similar approach?

Oddly enough, some women regard these unkempt male colleagues as kind of endearing and cute. Talk about maintaining double standards!

When picking an outfit, the key word is "appropriate." Don't try to look really cool if the other women don't. Check out the informal dress code by observing the deportment of your female leaders. Take your cue from them. Tummy or underwear display is never a good idea for anyone who wants to be taken seriously, and heels only make you look like you're lurching when you move quickly. A good rule of thumb: dress like you are already at the next management level. It makes you look like you're ready for that promotion.

3. Weight remains an issue. Maybe it's old-fashioned given how overweight the average person is today, but when looking for the next generation of leaders, most bosses still choose those they perceive to be physically fit and in control of their bodies. And unfair as it is, it's easier for men to get away with being overweight.

4. Conversational skills are a real asset. Those in the executive suite place great importance on your ability to speak to others in a clear, crisp, engaging manner. While the bosses I talk to don't believe that how you say something is as important as what you say, they rank verbal communication skills very highly. So much so that a lack of these skills can stop your advancement regardless of your results.

5. Good presentations and written messages can get you noticed. The ability to present in front of a group remains one of those less-well-recognized influencers of presence. Rehearse your presentation at least twice before you stand up in front of an audience. Written skills are also important, especially if you work in an organization with offices all over the place. Concise, articulate messages can really help differentiate you from the others issuing emails all day long.

Tips for Improving the Packaging

- In a perfect world we wouldn't judge anyone by the clothes they wear. But we don't live in a perfect world, and we certainly don't work in one. The clothes you wear are a reflection of who you are, what you stand for, and what you think about yourself and your position in the corporation.

- Your office, even if it's a cubby, is also a reflection of who you are, what you think about yourself, and how you view your own position. Have you ever walked into an office and immediately known—just from the décor and lighting—what kind of person you were about to meet? Whether they were going to be friendly or somber, open or serious? The same holds true for you! When someone enters your office, her very first impression won't be of you, but the setting. Your office reflects your personality. Now that you know this, you can use your office décor to influence what your new visitors think about you.

- You may not be the friendliest person on earth, but if you need your visitors, clients, or associates to think you're friendly, then let your office do most of the work for you. Make your office a friendly space with bright colors and flowers. Or, if your position requires you to be firm and precise when you are not a firm and precise person, let your office décor set the stage. You'll win half the battle before your visitor lays eyes on you.

Tips for Improving the Packaging

- Looking successful often creates more success. Even if moving into a nice office or dressing more professionally takes you out of your comfort zone, it is the right career move. Your company will expect you to put forth an image consistent with your position when meeting with clients, customers, and peers. And the image you project can help you close new deals, negotiate a better salary, or get your ideas taken seriously. A lack of presence at this juncture could cause you to be held back later on.

- Don't confuse looking and acting the part with being ostentatious and over the top. Remaining authentic is always a positive trait, so find a way to remain true to yourself.

Chapter 10

NOT GETTING A MENTOR

"The victory of success is half won when one gains the habit of setting goals and achieving them. Even the most tedious chore will become endurable as you parade through each day convinced that every task, no matter how menial or boring, brings you closer to fulfilling your dreams."

Og Mandino
Author and speaker

Women looking to advance in the business world, and *especially* those in a junior position, should get a mentor. This is a powerful and effective way for anyone in business to learn a variety of personal and professional skills.

Most of us can identify a person in our lives—a parent, friend, teacher, priest—who at some point had a significant and positive impact on us. This is the crux of mentoring. Many women might say, "I am smart and resourceful. Why do I need a mentor?" The answer is, anything ethical that can bring you closer to fully realizing your career goals is worth pursuing. And a smart, resourceful person will instantly discover what a wonderful resource a mentor can be.

Most often, a mentor is a person older and more experienced than you. It can be someone from within your corporation or someone in your industry with whom you have a telephone and email relationship. It can even be a man. As a matter of fact, a man on a very successful career track can be a real help.

Working as a role model, guide, catalyst, and cheerleader, your mentor can help you hone leadership skills, become more organized, deal with challenges, and develop a networking system. Once you figure out what areas you would like to improve, your mentor can begin working with you.

"Anna" was a tough-minded, hardworking, successful executive within the cosmetics business. Because she lacked a degree, she recognized that she had shortcomings which could hurt her career. She overcame this by aligning herself with a male executive significantly senior to her in both years and position. She let him know that she wanted to get ahead and would like him to show her the ropes. He did that. In private meetings they reviewed the company culture. In public meetings, he took her side and helped others to see that she was coming up with great ideas. It paid off for her.

Tips for Getting and Working with a Mentor

- Complete your life plan first. The more clearly you can communicate your plans for improvement, the more a mentor can assist you.

- Look within your organization and within your industry. While you don't have to pick a person you know well, he or she should be someone you admire, and who has the experience to assist you. Most of us are flattered when approached for advice, and being asked to become a mentor is no different. If you can think of no one who is suitable within your organization or network, go online and find a mentoring program that will match you up with one.

- Working with a mentor doesn't have to be done in person.

- It's vital to recognize the time, effort, and valuable input your mentor contributes. Developing mutuality will be important for sustaining your relationship, and one good way to reciprocate is to listen and follow through on advice. The mentor's reward is your success and respect.

- A relationship with a mentor isn't meant to last a lifetime. You may only want to work with a particular mentor to resolve a particular problem. When your goals change, your current mentor may no longer be the best person to help you.

- Always be prepared for mentoring sessions. Know what you want to accomplish. Inform your mentor about your progress. You must be an active participant in the relationship.

Chapter 11

ACTING LIKE A GIRL INSTEAD OF A WOMAN

"When a man gets up to speak, people listen, then look. When a woman gets up, people look; then, if they like what they see, they listen."

Pauline Frederick
Author

I've never heard a CEO giggle. I doubt very many people have. Being giggly is a bad thing for any woman trying to work her way up the corporate ladder.

Linguist Deborah Tannen, in a study she conducted for her book *You Just Don't Understand: Women and Men in Conversation,* found that women laugh 126 percent more often than men. And unfortunately, this laughter is not relegated to personal life.

Young girls giggle, not mature leaders. Doing so is a sign of nervousness and self-consciousness. I've heard many women giggle a bit just after saying something, and it diminishes the impact of what they have said. Both the message and its messenger become less credible.

Giggling aside, being overly humorous is not the best approach you can take if you're a woman who wants to be taken seriously within your organization. Even when the men in your group kid around, it's a good idea to tone down your involvement. For men, humor is an easy way of appearing to be involved with subordinates without actually having to be involved. When a boss acts funny or playful, he's not showing care or affection. As we've discussed, it's not personal.

Another common pitfall is being overly familiar in email. One executive I know was floored when she received an email message from a potential client, one she hadn't met or spoken to, that was similar in tone to the ones her teenage daughter wrote: "I'm soooooo glad you emailed. My computer crashed and I lost all your contact information." My executive friend was delighted with this reply as it clearly indicated to her who would have the upper hand in this business relationship.

Or the banker who sent an email to her new clients that began, "WOW! Thank you for all of your business!!!" Excessive use of exclamation marks, flowery borders, and smiley faces belong on personal correspondence, not business correspondence.

Ever gone for lunch with a friend who just can't make up her mind about what to order, or wants the restaurant to make a lot of substitutions? This sort of thing will send all the wrong messages during a business meal. Men generally don't worry about what they're going to eat and neither should women. If you can't decide on a simple lunch order, how can you be trusted to make critical business decisions? Choose your meal quickly, with a minimum of fuss, and then you can get down to business.

If alcohol is served at your business function, don't overindulge. Nothing screams "girl" more than being tipsy or, worse, drunk. Don't try to keep up with the men. Put your hand over your wine glass or, if you're hosting the event, speak to a member of the staff ahead of time to make sure they go lightly on your refills. Make sure you have plenty of water and drink lots of it.

Tips on How Not to Act Like a Girl

- Giggling is hard to consciously control, but control it you must. It has the same effect that qualifying your statements does—it negates the idea. If you have something to say, tell yourself ahead of time that you will end your sentence with a period, not a giggle. As with much self-defeating behavior, practice, diligence, and time will crack it.

- For some, giggling is a stress-relieving habit. If this sounds like you, it will be beneficial to find the underlying reasons for your stress and discover ways to alleviate it in a more productive fashion.

- When your boss gets playful with you, you can smile and acknowledge the humor, but don't get lured in. You have to find a balance between not insulting him and maintaining your professional demeanor.

- When shaking hands, make sure your grip is firm.

- Treat email correspondence with the same care as a memo written on paper. No smiley faces.

- Whether overcome with happiness, anger, or sadness, don't cry in the office. Go for a walk, go to the washroom, go to your car, but don't cry in the office. Executives don't cry.

- Don't chew gum.

- Choose your office decorations carefully. No Barbie memorabilia—unless you are the CEO of Mattel.

Chapter 12

GETTING CAUGHT UP IN OLD-BOY STEREOTYPES

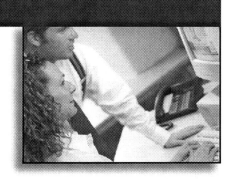

"I was blessed with a birth and a death, and I guess, I just want some say in between."

Ani DiFranco
Composer, business executive, and musician

Despite the progress we have made toward equal rights, women still cite men's preconceived beliefs about their roles and abilities as one of the strongest barriers to their advancement. Having seen so much of this firsthand, I can confirm that gender stereotyping is endemic to a lot of corporations and business organizations. It's actually the source of many jokes when the women have left the room. It's not easy for women to deal with and not easy to resolve.

There are some in our society (and not just men) who might say, "Well, it's been this way for a long time—why worry about it now? And why should I care?"

The answers to those questions can be as complex as the universe or as simple as this:

When colleagues or superiors rely on stereotypes to form opinions about your capabilities, the false assumptions they start out with will almost always lead them to erroneous conclusions. You will be seen as less worthy than your male counterparts in a number of ways, and this can be devastating to your career.

That's the bad news. The good news is that knowing just a few key things can prevent the perceptions of the old boys in their corner offices from doing you harm.

In her great book *Play Like a Man, Win Like a Woman*, author and executive Gail Evans discusses the issue of gender stereotyping very clearly. I will paraphrase her thoughts here and add some of my own. I encourage you to take the time to read her book.

Evans's observation is this: Most men enter the workforce with little experience of women as anything other than sisters, mothers, wives, and girlfriends. It's rare for them to have female best friends. As one might expect, a young boy spends a lot of time playing with other boys, and from his experiences he learns certain lessons about how to behave. As the boy becomes an adult, he carries these lessons with him. Now, the same is true of girls, of course. They too learn about how to act through their association with other girls. But the lessons are different. And therein lies a key determinant of how men and women interact later on in the workplace.

As Gail Evans notes, boys often experience a dimension of life that many girls never do—sports. In general, traditionally masculine sports are usually exclusive to boys. There is very little opportunity for boys to interact with girls while playing boy-type sports.

So when men enter the workplace and start working with women as peers, or employees, or supervisors, they have a tendency to assume that they occupy an identifiable role, or that they possess certain characteristics. Men who see women as passive, reluctant to take risks, or incapable of making tough decisions won't want to see more women around the boardroom table. And their perceptions will have a big impact on how they treat women in their business dealings.

To these men, all women are daughters, moms, wives, or lovers. It's unfortunate, but you need to be aware of it. I've seen a lot of very bright, talented, well-educated women have their careers derailed or stalled because they tried to be treated like one of the boys when, in truth, the boys saw them in one of these stereotypical roles.

Different stereotypical roles require different mindsets, and different strategies to overcome them. Evans notes:

- If you are seen as a daughter, you may be invited to high-level organizational meetings and introduced to influential people that others in your organization may not be privy to. You will, of course, also be privy to conversations and information that others at your level are not. But there is a downside to this particular scenario. You'll never be seen by "Daddy" as his equal, and this will become increasingly frustrating. Many male senior execs who think they are helping the company by promoting women are, in essence, treating them like daughters.

- If the man sees you in the same light as he sees his wife, you are treated as an almost-equal. You'll be part of high-level discussions and be given access to information that otherwise might not be part of your job description. On the downside, he may transfer all the crappy things he sees in his wife to you. So if he thinks she's a long-winded, boring individual, he may be inclined to tune you out when he's asking for everyone's input. If he regards his wife as a nag, you may get a very uncalled-for, snappish response to a request because he's transferring his perception of that naggy attitude to you.

- If he sees you as a mom figure, you may become responsible for all the company's nurturing activities, relegated to writing policy and handling personnel problems. You'll most likely have a job for life. The downside is that you'll never have as much power as others at the same level. Everyone will think of you as the boss's trusty assistant and confidante, but never allow you to develop into a truly important member of the team.

- Finally, if you are younger and more aggressive than other women he encounters, he's more likely to see you as the lover or mistress. It's a dangerous role for a couple of reasons. While you'll get to be a risk-taker and make decisions, you will also be walking a tightrope of sexual tension, and very few people know themselves well enough not to get tripped up. The consequence may be the loss of your job for something that wouldn't have happened if you were male.

To overcome these stereotypes, you have to behave like an executive at all times. Don't let yourself play the role of daughter, mother, wife, or mistress.

Here's an extreme example of how occupying a stereotypical role can spell disaster. "Elizabeth" was an attractive, assertive senior vice president in a large international firm. She had been promoted very quickly—perhaps beyond her ability and training—because she had been having an affair with the company's (married) CEO. He had seen her as the mistress type, and instead of keeping their relationship professional, she responded to his advances.

The affair ended, and when the business Elizabeth was overseeing started to flounder, she could no longer go to the CEO for advice. Her immediate supervisor was no help as he knew about their relationship, believed Elizabeth had been trying to sleep her way to the top, and felt she was getting what she deserved.

So, what can you do to avoid being stereotyped? Here are a few ideas:

Tips on Understanding and Working Around the Old Boy Stereotypes

- First, and perhaps most importantly, simply be aware of these stereotypes. Understand that, rightly or wrongly, they do exist and there is very little if anything that you can do to erase the lessons that these men learned as youngsters.

- Accept the fact that men do not, and in some cases *cannot*, see women in the same light as they do other men. In a perfect world, we would all be equals. One's efforts would be judged according to their merits and nothing else. But we don't live in a perfect world. Biases exist and unfair treatment occurs, and you have to recognize and deal with these things on a personal level.

- If you feel that this kind of stereotyping is prevelant in your work environment, identify the role in which your coworkers see you and devise a strategy that best suits your needs. Getting others to perceive you as your own person with your own credentials is the key. It's not easy, and but it can be done.

- Though you need to be conscious of potential stereotyping, don't assume that *all* men will be guided and influenced by these stereotypes. Many men—and their numbers are growing with each generation—are fair-minded and progressive. They will believe that a woman's input is as vital to a company's goals as another man's.

- Instead of wasting time and energy trying to correct someone's opinion about you or your style, understand how the old boys perceive women. Interpret their treatment of you as a male personality disorder, and then make it work to your advantage.

Chapter 13

NOT ACTING LIKE A POWER BROKER

"It really is a game, but few women recognize it as such. Women often don't see an overall strategy; that's why they don't recognize the game."

From "Working Around and Through the Old Boy's Network"
A BusinessSuccessCoach.net group coaching program

Power brokers are people who get things done. They accomplish what others cannot, regardless of position, status, or title. They are able to do this because they know how to play the game.

If there's more than one person working in your office, then there are politics and games to contend with. In a competitive environment, it's human nature to compete and jostle for attention, praise, position, and reward. What's at stake is a raise, the plum project, or a promotion.

The rules are mostly unwritten and you can only learn them as you go along, picking up information through alliances, networking, and keen observation. You win the game if you can advance your career with the fewest burned bridges.

If this sounds like a game you'd rather opt out of, think again. You have to play to get ahead. And the only reason you'd rather not play, most likely, is that you don't know how.

Men learn as young boys how to play competitive sports, constantly pushing the football or hockey coach to decide that they are the best. The hierarchy is clear. The coach is the boss, with the team captain or quarterback also in a position of leadership. And the name of the game is winning. Even when pulled out of the game because they screwed up, boys learn early on how to convince the coach that a second chance is in order. If the team wins and one of the boys was instrumental in making that happen, his accomplishment is rewarded with praise and recognition. So, years later, when men enter the workforce, they already have a great deal of experience in promoting their abilities.

Most women over thirty-five lack this early indoctrination into the competitive world unless they were brought up as sports enthusiasts. For the most part, today's businesswomen grew up in more nurturing environments where winning wasn't the point. The point was to participate and have fun, with no one leaving sad or hurt. Consensus-building was a primary skill they learned, as there was often no hierarchal leader. It's no wonder that they arrive at the office without game-playing skills in place.

Any company is a living, changing entity, adapting to its economic environment and growing or shrinking at an irregular pace. You have to be able to adapt with the company. You must prove yourself a viable player as it grows and changes so you can remain a part of its growth. Opting out of office politics and games is just not an option if you want to get ahead.

But being a player doesn't mean you have to partake in back-stabbing, rumor-mongering, or other unethical activities. Positive aspects of game-playing entail developing good people and communication skills, being diplomatic, cooperating, making important contributions, and promoting yourself. With a good understanding of your workplace culture, you can adjust your behavior and work habits in a way that keeps you in the game without betraying your values or causing yourself an undue amount of stress.

Case in point: I worked with an executive who was one of the few female vice presidents in her company. At first, people didn't pay much attention to her. She was in a staff department and those on the line side were too busy to give her comments any thought. "Stephanie" gradually became one of the most powerful people in the company, with many seeking her advice. How did she do it? She made frequent presentations at the monthly management meeting, and without exception her presentations were well prepared and full of thought-provoking material. She presented ideas that her colleagues could take action on, ensured that they were assigned to the appropriate line executive, and followed up at the next meeting to ensure that items were completed. She was articulate and presented her arguments in a lively, persuasive manner. She never made it personal and she always sat at the table. Soon no major decisions were made without her input.

If you want to investigate this issue in greater detail, I suggest an excellent book written by Lois P. Frankel, PhD: *Nice Girls Don't Get the Corner Office: 101 Unconscious Mistakes Women Make That Sabotage Their Careers*. The president of Corporate Coaching International, Dr. Frankel uses many real-world examples to introduce concepts and ideas. Her book is a great tool for any woman who wishes to build her career in a thoughtful and methodical manner.

Tips on Becoming a Recognized Power Broker

- Keep your eyes and ears open to what is going on around you. Listen to what people say and absorb what they mean.

- Learn how to communicate well with others at all levels.

- Start watching a competitive team sport. "Carley," a woman who co-owned a Toronto communications firm, observed that watching NFL football is the ideal way to get into the heads of the guys you work with—not to see who wins or loses, but to better understand teamwork and quarterbacking.

- Learn the unwritten rules. Some of the more obvious ones have to do with acceptable dress. I don't mean what's in the dress code, but what senior executives actually wear to work. Is the style conservative or contemporary? Does this vary by department? Less obvious is the identification of the true power brokers. Notice how some managers never seem to have problems getting people's attention at meetings. Notice how their ideas and suggestions are readily adopted even though they many not be the most senior in the group. These are the people with power.

- Discern which people you need to develop strategic relationships with, and nurture those relationships.

- Don't participate in the rumor mill. If you hear something, don't pass it on.

Tips on Becoming a Recognized Power Broker

- Be assertive without being aggressive.

- Take on leadership roles when possible so you can demonstrate your management abilities.

Chapter 14

HELPING MEN WHO ARE LESS COMPETENT

"So little done, so much to do."

Cecil Rhodes
Business magnate

All too often, I've watched competent, even competitive women try to help their male peers when they seem to be in distress. The help-seeking men tend to be rather lovable—maybe cute in a puppy dog kind of way—making it difficult to deny them the help they're asking for. I call this the I-Know-He's-a-Useless-Piece-of-Work-but-He's-My-Useless-Piece-of-Work syndrome. Men are not as prone to this.

In reality, the guy you want to help may not be a useless piece of work at all, but someone who is going through a bad time, or simply isn't skilled enough to complete his current project. But whatever the reason for his poor performance, you should consider distancing yourself if you are serious about your own career goals.

While the urge to help is kind and noble, it does nothing to advance your career. As a matter of fact, helping those who are less compe-tent can actually have a negative effect: others will see you in an unfavorable light due to your mere association with the badly per-forming individual.

The inclination to take on the added responsibility of helping a strug-gling coworker can come from a tendency to value community, the urge to mother, and professional courtesy. Though none of these things are bad in and of themselves, indulging a mothering urge in the office will interrupt your work, distract you from your immediate and long-range goals, and diminish your level of productivity and focus. It's part of the "my needs last" sensibility all too common among caregivers. This is probably not a healthy approach in the home, and it's certainly inappropriate in the office.

Women's superior ability to multitask may also come into play here, enabling you to feel that you can handle the extra time and effort involved in assisting a peer. Don't be fooled. This kind of person can take up an enormous amount of your time if you let him. Even if he's not consciously taking advantage of you, he's often a user, someone who will take what he can get from you whenever he can get it.

It may be hard to do, but you must leave the urge to teach, protect, and keep others from harm out of the office. Leave "Mother" at home, where your nurturing instincts can be put to better use.

Taking on the helper role can be a drain, and an extremely stressful one at that. Rewards are usually nonexistent and certainly irrelevant to the achievement of your career objectives. Your colleague's project might come to depend upon you more and more, with nobody giving you proper recognition for your help. Just as snakes, by their very nature, will bite because they can't stop themselves, these help-seekers will suck you dry if you let them.

Over the course of my many years in the corporate arena, I've seen women become negatively associated with the ones they help, killing any hope for advancement. It's the halo effect in reverse, and it's difficult to counter once it's in play.

Tips for Women Who Like to Help

- Get a good handle on what your responsibilities are, as well as what your goals are.

- Be discerning about who you choose to make alliances with.

- Set up criteria for knowing where legitimate teamwork ends and helping begins.

- Learn to say no. You can keep an inventory of reasons in your head that you can call upon, like, "If I do this with you, I won't meet my own deadline."

- Working with one of your employees is different than supporting a peer. If a member of your team is unproductive, you need to take action.

Chapter 15

FAILING TO PUT A SCREWUP IN PERSPECTIVE

"Men often become what they believe
themselves to be. If I believe I cannot do
something, it makes me incapable of
doing it. But when I believe I can, then I acquire the ability to do it even
if I didn't have it in the beginning."

Mohandas Gandhi
Visionary leader of India's independence

Every one of us has been a victim of harsh criticism at work. Even if
you are doing your job with great conviction and energy, criticism
for a screwup—or even a job done less well than expected—is inevitable.

In all the offices I've worked in over my thirty years in corporate
life, I've noticed that women have a harder time putting a screwup
in perspective and moving on. As competitive athletes, boys learn
how to butt heads and then pat each other on the back. A game, in
the end, is only a game—there's another one next week. Women, on
the other hand, tend to feel as though there is no hope for recovery.
They have not pleased their boss, word is going to spread, and the
axe is going to drop.

Women feel the need to do good work more keenly than men.
Remember, it's the women who feel their work should speak for
them. So it's no wonder that when something goes wrong, their
world caves in.

Screwing up does not mean you are a bad manager, or that you're not doing a good job overall. And it does not mean you will be let go. It means you screwed up this time, so do better in the future. Don't aim for perfection; you'll be disappointed every time.

No one wants to be on the receiving end of criticism, but when you mess up a project or assignment, there is a lot to be gained if you handle the comments professionally. Regardless of whether the criticism is constructive, it becomes your job to face the situation without becoming defensive. Remember, it's not personal. But it is imperative that you learn how to cope with criticism and learn how to put it in perspective. How effectively you respond will have an impact on your professional growth and ultimate success.

There is a quote from President Abraham Lincoln that has helped me through tough times. He said, "I do the best I know how, the very best I can. I mean to keep on doing this, down to the very end."

Tips on Coping with a Screwup

- Listen to the criticism. Though you may feel hurt, even devastated, try to see past your emotions to the task at hand. You need to work through this. And whatever you do, don't cry. Just as "there's no crying in baseball," there's no crying in the workplace.

- Don't become defensive. Instead, make sure you understand the criticism, and ask questions if you feel you need to better grasp where you went wrong and what you need to do to rectify the situation. Ask your supervisor exactly what it is she did not like and why. Then ask how she would improve things.

- If you did something wrong, be honest and admit it. You will gain respect for this. Work with your boss to arrive at a consensus on what you should do next and then do it in a timely manner.

- If you notice the problem before your boss does, make him aware of it and, at the same time, present a solution. Better yet, implement the solution prior to meeting with your boss.

- Forget the criticism. Dwelling too long on your mistake or shortcomings will only make you less useful.

- Get together with colleagues to discuss what happened and get their assessments. Often, what it felt like to you is entirely different from how it will appear to others who can be more objective. Bonus tip: try to get a few men in these review dialogs—we're far less bothered by such situations.

Chapter 16

FAILING TO BLOW OFF STEAM

"If you always do what you've always done, you'll always get what you've always gotten."

From the Sedona Method

Women tend to bottle things up. Thinking you can cope, believing your strong feelings will pass, you may brush conflict off to the side. But over time, keeping those feelings in causes resentment, making you feel more negative about your company, those you work with, and your job in general. Pent-up anger can also lead to unhealthy levels of stress and contribute to burnout. Carrying around all that negativity makes you less desirable for a promotion or transfer.

Everyday frustrations, while inevitable, need not ruin your workday, your health, or your career. Blowing off steam is a good tool for dealing with them, allowing you to get on with your job and tolerate the more irritating people you need to interact with.

Note that by "blowing off steam," I don't mean whining to your colleagues about your tribulations. That will only make you more cranky. But discussing the frustrating situation with others can give you perspective and help you learn from it. Confronting the source of conflict in a professional, calm manner can also be constructive.

Physical activity is another great way to blow off steam. Many businesspeople set aside a certain amount of time to go for a run, do Pilates, play volleyball, meditate, get a massage, etc.

Tips on How to Appropriately Release Pressure at Work

- Understand your corporate culture and use it as a guide. For instance, is most information in your office conveyed formally, in memos and scheduled meetings, or is email the norm? Follow the existing conventions of your office when you communicate.

- Writing can be a good way to blow off steam. Just don't send the letter or email in the heat of the moment. Sleep on it and see if it still makes sense in the morning.

- Learn about your coworkers' and supervisor's personality traits and find out what sets them off. Also learn what behavioral characteristics they have that set you off.

- Resist getting involved in conflicts that don't directly involve you.

- Depersonalize conflicts.

- Make your complaints or desires known in a straightforward and direct way. Never whine about how you weren't included in a meeting. Instead, state assertively that you want to be included in any future meetings.

- Try to resolve conflicts with coworkers without involving your superiors. If you go to them, they may get the impression that you are unable to solve problems on your own.

Tips on How to Appropriately Release Pressure at Work

- If certain managers are frequent sources of conflict for you, and you need to have a good working relationship with them to meet your goals, spend more time with them. Make a concentrated effort to improve communication.

- Reiterating what a coworker is saying to you is a good way to avoid misunderstandings. Not only will you ensure that you understand exactly what he is saying to you, but it will also make him feel he's being heard.

- Don't talk to others about an office conflict if they are not involved.

General tips for reducing stress and pressure:

- Find a relaxation method that works for you. Some good outlets are yoga, meditation, hobbies, and socializing. In a pinch, even breathing deeply for a minute or two while sitting at your desk will help slow your mind down and allow you to think more clearly.

- Keep yourself physically healthy by eating well and taking vitamins. At the very least your body will be better able to manage the stress.

- Get involved in a sport or exercise regularly. The release of endorphins is a natural stress-fighter.

Chapter 17

SHRINKING AWAY FROM NEGOTIATION

"I'm tough, I'm ambitious, and I know exactly what I want. If that makes me a bitch, okay."

Madonna
Singer, business executive, and performer

Negotiation is a process many women shy away from, primarily because they are uncomfortable about asking for what they want. Most women I've met in my coaching practice have not created a life plan, which leads me to believe that they don't know what they want. If you have no idea where you want to be in one year or in five, how can you effectively negotiate for any particular outcome?

Some women are also less aware than they should be of what others within their organization or industry are making. You should know that men talk about their salary and benefits. It's almost a hobby for the really competitive ones. Women, on the other hand, do not. When it's time for the annual raise or bonus, they are more likely to passively accept what is offered to them. As discussed elsewhere here, they often downplay their accomplishments. In many ways women sometimes become unwitting partners in the persistence of unequal pay.

Women's tendency not to negotiate may also mean that they fail to gain the experience they need to reach the upper levels of management. There's a tendency to limit our view on what's negotiable to salary and benefits, but you can—and should—negotiate for whatever you think you need to meet your goals: opportunities for business travel, specific positions within the company, staff, resources, and educational opportunities.

One successful executive I worked with, "Sarah," was finding it difficult to balance her professional life with her home life, which consisted of a husband and three children. She felt the only option available to her was to resign. She came to speak to me about her decision, and it became clear that she was undervaluing her contribution to the company and uncomfortable selling her accomplishments. After we spoke, she worked on a presentation to her boss. Instead of resigning from the company, she was able to negotiate a significant increase in the amount of time she could work from home and a computer on which to work. Talk about a win-win.

Negotiating is a skill that comes with a lot of emotional baggage. You have to apply other difficult skills I've spoken about, like self-promotion and speaking up. Add to this just how risky it feels to make yourself vulnerable to your superiors, and it's no wonder women unhappily accept what comes their way instead of asking for what they've rightfully earned. If you know you're making less money than a male colleague, and your skills and experience appear to be equal, you owe it to yourself to take your case to your supervisor or human resources. You will not only be helping yourself, but also helping to create a more egalitarian workplace.

While socialization and cultural norms often interfere with a woman's willingness to negotiate, you can overcome them by learning the required skills to negotiate successfully.

Tips on Negotiating Successfully

- Preparation is key for any good negotiation. Gather as much information as you can about what you're going to negotiate. If it's a salary and benefits package, ask coworkers about their pay or stock options. Talk to your human resources department; they may be able to provide you with all sorts of information about your company and refer you to external sources. Good HR managers want to help retain executives and keep abreast of industry trends. You can research what others in comparable positions earn at public companies.

- Try to learn about the person you'll be negotiating with too. The more you know, the better off you are. When you show the other party that you are well-informed, he may come to think you know more than you actually do.

- Try to make the negotiation impersonal. If it will give you the confidence to push for what's fair, imagine that you are a hired negotiator working on someone else's behalf.

- Know what your plan is: what's your bottom line, when would you walk away from a deal, what are you willing to trade, etc.

- Know your accomplishments and use numbers to back you up. If you've increased sales by 30 percent or doubled your productivity in the last year, demonstrate it by working out exact figures. Being a loyal employee is not enough, and neither is needing the money. To justify your request, you need to demonstrate how the thing you're asking for will benefit the company, not just you.

Tips on Negotiating Successfully

- Time your meeting wisely. If quarterly figures have just come in and they don't look so hot, or your supervisor is experiencing some problems of her own, waiting might be best.

- Practice your negotiation skills both at and away from work. Try them on your family when you want some chores done. The more you get what you want, the better you'll feel about asking for it.

- Read a book on how to improve your negotiation skills. There are plenty of resources online and at your local library.

Chapter 18

ACTING TOO AGGRESSIVE

"I am feeling very lonely right now. Nobody is fighting for me."

Hillary Rodham Clinton
U.S. senator and former first
lady

An executive I worked with, "Alexandra," was climbing the corporate ladder quickly. Bright and talented, she had all the executive presence one person could have, and she used it thoughtfully. She was very savvy, worked hard, and dressed in the best designer wear. Although still relatively young, she'd become the first COO of a large retail chain.

On her way through the ranks she'd modeled the behavior of the other successful executives—almost entirely male—in the corporation. As a result, she picked up a few stereotypically masculine habits. She was known for being rather foul-mouthed when it wasn't necessary, and for being very hard on her underlings—especially in public forums. While respected for her career achievements, she was strongly disliked. Men considered her a bitch. Women resented her vulgarity, which they saw as unbecoming, and believed that her behavior reflected badly on the other female executives.

When things got tough, the other managers did not support their female boss. In fact, most of them clearly wanted her gone ASAP. They got their wish. Why did the behavior that gave her male peers a reputation for being tough-minded cause her demise?

Any woman who has been in the workplace for a few years has learned that when a woman behaves aggressively she's the "B-word," while a man who acts the same way is perceived as strong. Men are used to being aggressive with other men. They grew up on games like football and have been trained to think that aggression is synonymous with taking care of business. They have also been brought up to believe that women are not tacklers and fullbacks.

This means that when a woman behaves aggressively, men don't like it. And when a woman blows up, they think it's downright scary. Psychologists tell me this has a lot to do with male fear of the feminine. For anyone who wishes to examine this concept more fully, I recommend *The Heroine's Journey: Woman's Quest for Wholeness* by Maureen Murdoch. Written in 1990, it's required reading in many post-secondary psychology and therapy programs. Her thoughtful work makes for a very interesting assessment of the issues that crop up between the sexes at work on a daily basis.

So, in an office culture where the men are getting things done the good ol' boys' way—by bumping heads and jostling for position—how can you achieve? Women who find a good balance, being assertive and strong without scaring the men off, will do best.

Tips on Being Assertive, Not Aggressive

- Speak up and be direct.

- Stand up straight and make eye contact.

- Experiment to find the right assertion equation for the men
  in your office. Somewhere right in between steamroller and
  doormat lies the right mix of gumption that will get the guys'
  attention. It's possible to let them know you're a player without
  inadvertently causing them to tune you and your contributions
  out.

Chapter 19

FAILING TO MAKE THE REQUIRED INVESTMENT

"I am woman! I am invincible! I am pooped!"

Author Unknown

It's 5 p.m. The boss calls, asking you and a male colleague to join him for a brief meeting. What's the first thing you do: grab pen and paper and head over, or pick up the phone to adjust your child care arrangements? What do you think your male colleague's response is? Who will be more relaxed and focused at the meeting? Who will make a better impression with the boss?

If you want to be promoted to the most senior levels, the simplest advice I can give you is, don't get married and don't have children. Not very realistic, I know, so be prepared to make significant invest- ments that most men don't have to make to ensure your home life runs smoothly without you. Without adequate support on the domestic front, you likely won't be promoted to CEO. Caring for a family is hard work. Running a business is hard work. Men don't even think of trying to do both and neither should you.

To reach the pinnacles of corporate success, business has to be your all-consuming passion and your number one priority. That's what it takes, and you can be sure your equally ambitious male colleagues will be eating and breathing business in their quest for success. If you don't want to run the company, then look at what executives at the level you aspire to are doing. Are twelve-hour days and weekend conference calls the norm? Then that's what will be expected of you.

Not everybody wants to be a senior executive, but if becoming the CEO is your dream, then you're going to need significant help when it comes to taking care of your family. Be prepared to hire a nanny, housekeeper, personal shopper, tutor, or gardener. Obtain the support you need to allow you to perform at your best.

Most families make decisions about such things on the fly, resulting in stress and, often, absences from work. One executive I worked with, "Gail," is the mother of one child. Her advancement into senior management coincided with her child's advancement at school, and as her child's life became busier and busier, Gail confided in me that it had been a mistake to not hire a nanny. The demands of juggling work and home eventually led to burnout, and Gail is no longer on the fast track.

Don't expect female executives to be more understanding of the strains that come with juggling career and motherhood. One young female executive, CEO of a large retail chain, was herself the mother of two young children. When conducting a performance review with one of her middle managers, her advice was blunt: if you want to become a senior executive, hire a nanny. The manager was a bit taken aback, but she realized her boss had given her a much-needed wake-up call. She needed to make an investment if she wanted to reach the ranks of senior executive. She couldn't be watching the clock at the end of the day, timing her departure with the closing of the day care facility.

In addition to dealing with the practical issues, be prepared for the emotional toll a career can take on a working mother. Being away from your children isn't easy and, generally speaking, senior executives work long days and travel regularly. Nightly phone calls to your family help you keep in touch when on the road, but may also trigger feelings of guilt as you're reminded that you're not there to tuck your little one in or help with a homework problem. Your male colleague may be missing his children too, but as society still views mothers as our children's primary caregivers, he isn't likely to be suffering from the same pangs of guilt.

In addition to working out the home-life issues, you also need to ensure that you're staying ahead of the game in terms of personal development. You have to keep your skills current, be aware of general trends in your industry, and, of course, know the scores from last night's game. Doing this requires a considerable investment of your time. This is work completed outside of work—and something that men have to do too. At last, some fair play in the workplace! A tip for success in this area is to hire a competent executive assistant who can schedule appropriate seminars and training courses as well as flag key news articles for your review.

Fact: Husbands of working women do approximately the same amount of work around the home as husbands of nonworking women.

Fact: Less than 4 percent of America's largest corporations are run by female CEOs.

Fact: Getting to the top is hard work and requires considerable investment, emotional and otherwise.

Tips on Making the Required Investment

- The successful businessperson in the twenty-first century realizes she needs to continually upgrade her skillset. Too many of today's managers are relying on the outdated tools and teachings they acquired in college. In many cases, they are becoming obsolete.

- It takes time to make money. As you become more successful, be aware that you may have less time to do the other things so important to a well-balanced life. Allow yourself to take a break once in a while or you risk becoming burned out. Meditation during the day is great for this.

- Invest in yourself. Consider using more assistance for "short-term catch-ups." This can include nannies, housekeepers, and gardeners for household help; financial managers or business coaches for business advice; and spiritual counselors or fitness coaches for personal growth.

- Remember, no one can do it all on their own. In the '80s many career women liked to joke that they needed a wife. There was some truth to the line.

- While away from loved ones, make use of technology to keep in touch and on top of things. But don't forget that personal presence is the key to all successful relationships. Email or voicemail can only maintain a relationship for a short while, and it can rarely build one of substance.

Chapter 20

VIEWING THE WORKPLACE AS HUSBAND-HUNTING COUNTRY

"Stop thinking about what you can achieve—think about what you can contribute. This is how you will achieve."

Peter Drucker
Author, teacher, and management guru

We spend so much time at work, it's only natural to envision the office as a good place to look for romance. After all, we know we already share a lot in common with our peers and even supervisors. But for many reasons, office affairs are a big mistake—more so for women than for men. As we've discussed, women tend to view their job as something that reflects their own personal values. Consequently, it is easy to expect that others they work with share those same values and ideals. This isn't necessarily the case. Don't expect your male (or female) colleagues to share your vision just because they work alongside you.

That said, the object of your attraction may still be willing to participate in certain extracurricular activities with you.

Having an affair with someone in your office is comparable to having one in a small town. Gossips, backstabbers, and those who would rather they get the next promotion instead of you will do their best to undermine your credibility.

As much as we'd like to think that times have changed, I'm here to tell you they haven't as far as sex is concerned. Sleeping with a coworker (or worse, your supervisor) is good for men and bad for women. Men acquire reputations as studs, women as easy.

An office relationship may interfere with your ability to perform your professional duties, or create the impression that it does.

Even if your company has no formal policy against intra-office dating, the stakes are too high, and the legal consequences potentially dev-astating. While we tend to think of women as being the victims of sexual harassment in the workplace, the law protects men too, and more of them are coming forward to register complaints. And if your affair begins to negatively affect others in your workplace, those people may also file a complaint against you. Between office gossips, your hurt pride, workplace policies, and sexual harassment legisla-tion, you really need to ask yourself if an office romance is worth jeopardizing your professional goals.

The fact that you spend so much time in the office is not a good reason to look for romance there—it's a good reason to avoid it at all costs. Any repercussions could adversely affect your career for years.

Tips on Steering Clear of Intra-office Relationships

- Relationships between coworkers are not seen as negatively as relationships between a manager and her boss (or his boss), but neither one is safe.

- Before you start an office relationship, consider the consequences of breaking up and how that will affect you.

- Also be wary of getting involved with someone who works for one of your company's suppliers, vendors, or competitors. In addition to the potential romantic pitfalls, you also risk people bringing your impartiality into question—regardless of the facts.

- Make time to meet people if finding romance is important to you. Sign up for a class or join a professional group.

- If someone from the office asks you out, simply be strong and let them know that you have a policy never to date anyone from the office. And stick to this policy.

Chapter 21

FALLING INTO WOMEN'S ROLES

"Avoiding danger is no safer in the long run than outright exposure. The fearful are caught as often as the bold."

Helen Keller
Lecturer and author

Throughout the course of history, women have been socialized to perform certain gender-specific roles. Although the opportunities for women to take on traditionally masculine roles have been increasing rapidly, the assumption that they will continue to be nurturers remains. This has left members of both sexes feeling confused and conflicted.

Even when a woman holds a position of relative power in the office, she is still usually the one who is responsible for most of the child care and household maintenance. Unsurprisingly, she will often slip back into the role she plays during her off hours, doing the domestic tasks and providing emotional support.

I've known a lot of highly qualified women who would always take it upon themselves to get the coffee, make everyone copies of reports, and keep the kitchen area stocked. They would even give coworkers a shoulder to cry on when troubles arose. Struggling for recognition and inclusion, they attempted to gain acceptance by taking on a caretaker role.

Everyone likes the support a caretaker provides—who wouldn't?

The problem is that while appreciated, that kind of support is not highly regarded. It assures that the people around you will take you for granted. And once your coworkers identify you as the caretaker, the role will be difficult to shed. You'll get the less desirable tasks, projects, and committees—the ones that are more frequently delegated to women. You'll also miss out on opportunities to prove yourself—business trips, for instance—because your superiors think a woman "wouldn't want to do that."

Willing to travel? Make sure your boss knows. Not willing to be your department's human resources representative? Say so, or negotiate that it be a temporary assignment. Go on record as not interested in the "opportunities" that can only lead to a dead end. And if you are on your way up the ranks, avoid caretaking like the plague.

Tips on Avoiding Traditional Roles

- If an undesirable task is forced upon you, try to negotiate some payback: "If I'm taking this project on, then I will need additional resources, changes to due dates ..."

- Volunteer for high-profile and difficult projects. Don't wait to be asked. If your boss declines your offer, calmly ask for some feedback and express your interest in being selected for the next big project. Don't assume your boss knows of your interest in tackling tough assignments.

- Do not volunteer to get coffee or make copies. Sit on your hands and bite your tongue if necessary. Do not make direct eye contact if a meeting participant asks for a volunteer—flip through papers, tie your shoe, or make yourself busy writing notes.

- If you already do the domestic duties, there is a way out. Announce to the group that you'd like the responsibility of stocking the kitchen to be shared, and that you will post a schedule that people can sign up for. Once that's in place, do not under any circumstances fill in, even if no one else volunteers. Let the office go coffee-less. You can bring in your own coffee from the outside.

- If you are the boss, then getting the coffee is actually a positive. It gives the message that you are comfortable with your power and position. Just don't do it every day.

References

Useful Resources

Business Success Coach.net	www.businesssuccesscoach.net
Business Woman Web	www.BusinessWomanWeb.com
John McKee	www.johnmmckee.com
Advancing Women	www.advancingwomen.com
National Organization for Women	www.now.org
Workopolis	www.workopolis.com/content/ resource/usablenews/women. html
Career Women	www.careerwomen.com
Vault.com	www.vault.com
Mind Tools	www.mindtools.com
Equal Employment Opportunity Commission	www.eeoc.gov
Sedona Method	www.sedonamethod.com

Bibliography

Play Like a Man, Win Like a Woman
   by Gail Evans, Broadway Books, © 2000

blink. The Power of Thinking Without Thinking
   by Malcolm Gladwell, Little Brown and Company, © 2005

*Nice Girls Don't Get The Corner Office: 101 Unconscious Mistakes
   Women Make That Sabotage Their Careers*
   by Lois P. Frankel, PhD, Warner Books, © 2004

Men are From Mars, Women Are From Venus
   by John Gray, HarperCollins, © 1992

You Just Don't Understand: Women and Men in Conversation
   by Deborah Tannen, HarperCollins, © 2001

The Heroine's Journey: Woman's Quest For Wholeness
   by Maureen Murdock, Shambhala Publications, © 1990

The Power of Intention
   by Dr. Wayne W. Dyer, Hay House, © 2004

Zen Mind, Beginner's Mind
   by Shyunryu Suzuki, Weatherhill Inc, © 1970

DEVELOPING A PERSONAL ACTION PLAN

Simple 9-Step Program

Congratulations on making a commitment to realizing your full potential. By looking objectively at your personal life with the same degree of focus normally reserved for business, you are about to begin the active management of all aspects of your life.

The 9-Step Program really works, but a word of caution is in order. Like all important activities, what you get out of it is directly proportional to what you put into each step. From experience, I can honestly promise that you will enjoy unprecedented levels of satisfaction and success if you proceed thoughtfully through your personal action plan. I've seen people experience profound and amazing changes in their lives as a result of the process you are about to undertake.

Consider some of their results:

- A business owner, previously fearful of making any changes in his life, went on to purchase a new home located across the country, sell his businesses, adopt a child, learn to ride a motorcycle, and begin a new career—all within a year of completing his plan.

- A senior executive received a nearly 200-percent increase in compensation, got a promotion, and moved to a new city, all within six months of completing her personal action plan.

- A woman who felt her life was out of control because she was dissatisfied on both the home and career fronts quickly checked off nearly all of her plan's first-year objectives, regaining her confidence, appearing on TV, and getting a promotion. Seven months after creating her plan, she felt energized and able to enjoy more quality time with her three children, casting aside much of the baggage she'd been carrying at home.

When first meeting very successful people, I make it a point to ask them for one tip or secret. Virtually all of these individuals tell me they have a clear plan for themselves that extends beyond their career. Studies indicate that 86 percent of individuals with a life plan rate their lives as satisfactory or very satisfactory. Compare that with the rest of the population. Compare it to yourself.

Background

Having a personal action plan keeps you on track to be the person you want to be. It helps to point out activities that derail you, and to realign you with your intention. In general, this type of plan helps to ensure that your life is the best possible.

If you are unclear about your goals and objectives, you are less likely to achieve them. If you are clear about where you are going, you are more likely to get there!

By the time most people reach the level of manager, they have created annual plans for their area of responsibility. This planning works because:

- We force ourselves to focus time and attention on the urgent, important business needs for the year ahead.

- We share the plans with others who are in a position to help us.

- We monitor our progress and react to results during the plan's time frame.

- We make appropriate changes and reforecast if necessary.

- We describe in our annual plan any and all activities we must engage in, or complete, to deliver multi-year projects.

As a coach, I frequently survey new clients by asking if they are more successful in their professional life or their personal life. *Nearly all people believe they are more successful in their career.*

A key reason for this is that most people don't *plan* their personal life.

I am about to present you with a choice. You can let life continue to just happen, or you can proactively plan and monitor it. Personal action planning works in the same way that planning your business does. Your plan will ensure that you will achieve more than you would have otherwise. Guaranteed.

The 9 Steps for Your Personal Action Plan

If you are not going to devote as much time and care to creating and managing your personal plan as you'd devote to your work, you should stop now. After all, this is your life we're talking about. Surely it's worth a few hours each year to ensure you are satisfied, growing, and positive about your direction, right?

I recommend using an item-by-item attack the first time you develop your action plan. This will ensure that you don't miss something in your planning and prioritization. Don't hesitate to challenge yourself. And it's OK to be a bit selfish about what you want. After all, there's no need to share this document with anyone else. I actually suggest that you don't. The people you care about, the ones you're most tempted to share your plans with, are often the first ones to tell you that your dreams are impossible. They will do this because they want to help you. They think that by getting you grounded in the "real world," you will stop fantasizing and get back to doing what you've been doing before. They don't mean to be negative, but their comments may be sufficient to stop you from pursuing those all-important steps that will take you to the next level.

This is a bit like trying to quit an addiction like smoking. There are those who advise that the person who wishes to quit go around telling everyone. The logic is that you'll embarrass yourself if you backslide. In my experience, this is rarely as effective as simply stopping, and not even mentioning it unless you're asked. And when asked, the best answer is that you haven't indulged for however many days/weeks/months so far, and you are taking it one day at a time because you know you could slip.

To sum up, pursue your goals aggressively and be positive. But don't set yourself up to feel like a failure if it takes a little longer to get there than you plan. I do believe a real support group is beneficial. This can consist of others doing the same thing, or a close friend who really wants to see you break records, or a professional like a coach whose only motivation is to help get you to the top of your game.

Plan what you really want in your life.
Then, manage your plan.

Step 1: Get to know the real you

I believe most people do what's expected of them—even when it conflicts with what they'd prefer to be doing. Every day we hear people say they don't like their jobs. Occasionally we hear people say they don't like their partners or spouses. Unfortunately, some people go further—they say they don't like themselves. All too often people tell us that they have "no choice" about how they live their lives, or that they simply "can't afford" to make any real change.

At the same time, individuals in all walks of life will tell us that the key to their success is that they are doing what they love. We hear businesspeople like Steve Jobs of Apple and Meg Whitman of eBay say it. Creative people like George Clooney, Julia Roberts, and Michael Crichton say it repeatedly. "Thought leaders" such as Oprah Winfrey, Martha Stewart, Dr. Wayne Dyer, and even Howard Stern say it as well.

But still, for many reasons, most people will tell you that you're living in a fairy-tale world if you believe you can do what you enjoy, make a good living, and still have time for yourself and your loved ones. I'd make a bet that those people have never taken the time to make a plan regarding how they want their life to go. If you agree, then you can understand why discussing your plans and goals with them is counterproductive. They've already decided it's unlikely that anyone can get what they want from life.

But you and I know better. Here's a statistic you might find interesting:

- Almost 80 percent of people never take the time to look at their life holistically.

Many of those same folks probably agree that having a budget for household spending is a good idea. Intellectually, they get the concept that planning can improve one's situation, at least regarding money (although whether they even do financial planning is questionable).

Each of us has things that we really care for. We know, even if only deep down inside, what makes us most satisfied. I believe it's worth the effort to create a plan for obtaining those things or doing those things. A good plan will allow you to measure your progress and will let you know when you're getting there. It will inspire you to stretch and test yourself as you move ahead. That makes you more interesting, and often more physically and mentally strong.

It's been said that each of us has two people residing in the same body: a social self that we present each day to the world, and an authentic self that tries to do what it loves and is naturally skilled at. The latter was labeled as our *psyche* by the famous psychoanalyst Carl Jung. Our authentic self and social self are often quite different from each other. Our authentic self may be buried deep within, rarely surfacing because it's not consistent with how we present ourselves to the world. Jung believed that as long as we don't examine our dreams and feelings, we are doomed to keep doing things that cause us a lot of heartburn.

Psyche - pronounced sike-ee
        - from the Greek meaning *breath, life, soul*
        - noun for the human soul, mind, or spirit

For our purposes, consider your authentic self to be your true self, or psyche. Its values define what you would be and do if you were free to proceed. To be both satisfied and successful, your authentic self is what should guide your ambitions, give you a sense of where you're going, and help you set goals.

- Without truly knowing your authentic self, you often find yourself feeling unsatisfied—even when you're successful. That's because your goals have been set according to your social self's values. They may have little real value for you.

So, if you want to be more satisfied, be more fit, be better off financially, or have better personal relationships, it's critical that your personal action plan takes your authentic self into account.

Tips on Understanding Your True Self

Here are a couple of questions to contemplate.

1. What would you love to be able to do if life put no constraints on you?

Examples of possible answers:

- If I could do anything I wanted, I'd travel the world and use the business skills I've learned to help people in developing countries become entrepreneurs.

- If I didn't have these responsibilities, I'd love to help children become more competitive by offering my services to the school board for free and teach classes that are not available.

- If I had been smarter I would have found a way to start my own Internet marketing business, and I would have made a fortune using a technology that feels natural to me.

2. If you awoke tomorrow and found that you had no demands from your spouse/partner, family, institutions, or job, and no monetary restrictions, what would you do?

Here are a couple more questions that might make you take a deep breath:

3. What was your favorite thing to do when you were an adolescent?

If it was creative, like writing or making music, and you now work in a factory-type environment where you just feed the machines or the computers around you, it's likely that you aren't feeling stimulated.

4. Think back to when you were a kid. What were you doing when you smiled the most? If it was playing outdoors, and now you find yourself in meetings all day, it's likely that you aren't feeling very passionate.

Without passion, as everyone knows, it's much harder to go the extra mile to become the best. When you're in touch with your authentic self, you will be more conscious of doing the things you're passionate about.

Step 2: Write a statement about your authentic self

Using your answers to the questions above, write a statement about who you are on the inside. Your statement should be brief, easy to remember, and easy to communicate. Later in this process, we will add details to reinforce it. For now, we just want it to be compelling.

Examples:

- I like to help other people.

- I am dedicated to having a very happy life.

- I show my children how to be successful and happy.

- I truly enjoy spending as much time as I can on the job.

- I do what I want, when I want.

When you are clear about who you are and what really motivates you, everything else will fall into place. You will be able to use your statement as your sherpa, something to help you navigate difficult waters—business meetings, relationships, ethical dilemmas, or whatever else life throws at you.

Step 3: Understand your vision and put it on paper

Once you've come up with an authentic-self statement that energizes you and focuses your sense of purpose, you express it through your vision. *Your vision is what you want for your life.*

Here are some examples of a vision statement:

- I mentor people to help them achieve their maximum potential.

- I travel to the places I want with people I enjoy.

- I set an example to my children so they see true happiness and strong values.

- I manage my financial affairs to ensure I have ample capital and cash flow.

Write down a vision statement for your life. This will drive your *strategy*—what you are going to do to satisfy your needs.

Vision connects our authentic self with specific goals. Consider an artist: her psyche may derive satisfaction from creating beautiful things; her vision may be to paint great works of art; specific goals get her vision to canvas. As we'll find in the following steps, it's easy to plot a course when we are committed to our vision, establishing appropriate short-term goals to attain it. This ensures that we satisfy our authentic self, and that our psyche is aligned with our social self.

Step 4: Identify the first goals that come to mind

Goal-setting is where the rubber hits the road. Those who fail to satisfy their authentic self usually do so because they try to get directly to their vision without taking short-term goals into account.

To identify your goals, *very quickly* write down all those things you'd love to accomplish, acquire, or become.

Be selfish. Put down anything and everything you'd get if life were perfect. Don't allow your common sense or the "real world" to get in the way of having some fun with this.

If you'd like to move to Italy, say so, even if you can't imagine how that's ever going to be possible. If you wish you had $1 million or no debts because that would help you sleep at night, write it down. A career change? Note it. Traveling to Thailand with a loved one to help rebuilding efforts for homeless people? Go for it! Nothing is off-base or inappropriate at this stage in your planning. This is simply a list of everything that you'd have and enjoy in a perfect world where your authentic self is supported by your vision.

Please, don't concern yourself with how long it takes to make the list. Write down all of your goals (try for twenty-five) and then separate them into the following categories:

- Personal/family

- Financial

- Career/professional

Within these categories you will note specifics such as possessions, wealth, business activities, career aspirations, fitness and weight issues, and others. How well you execute this exercise will determine how successful you are in realizing your vision, and living your essential self.

Step 5: Choose your most important goals

In each category, note the most important goals. Pull these to create a list of about ten. These are the items you'll want to accomplish within the next twelve months, to ensure that you live your vision statement.

You should be able to look at your short list and feel that you'll be very satisfied if you do nothing with the rest of your life except accomplish these goals.

Step 6: Prioritize your most important goals

Alert: this part is tough!

Take your short list and place the items in order of priority. Start by identifying the single most important goal on that list. If you could *only* do one thing in the next twelve months, where would you focus?

Now identify the next most important one.

Continue until you are satisfied with the order. You may become a little exhausted.

This step forces you to apply real-world thinking to your goals and, perhaps more importantly, your priorities. At this stage you may realize that your psyche and vision aren't aligned with others' demands. This is also the point where you come to realize that it is tough to change your existing behavior.

I hope you are now in too deep to abandon the creation of your personal action plan.

Now that you have your ordered key goals, merge the remaining lower-priority items from your original three categories to create a new list of multi-year goals. These are the ones you don't need to accomplish immediately to be happy.

Step 7: Set your timelines

Looking at the prioritized list of items you absolutely want to accomplish within twelve months, write a date for each goal to indicate when it will be accomplished or satisfied.

The date doesn't need to reflect the priority you assigned to the goal. As an example, just because you've noted that the most important thing you can do within a year is take a trip with your daughter to Delhi, that doesn't mean it has to be completed before lower-priority goals.

It is extremely important that target dates be attainable given everything you know about the things that will affect your ability to deliver on these promises to yourself.

Now do the same thing for the goals on your multi-year list. Again, it's very important that you really think the targets on the list appear reasonable and achievable. Otherwise, at some point in the future, you'll start giving up on achieving them. Really successful people understand that it takes time to get everything they want, while others try to accomplish everything very quickly and then fail.

Step 8: Monitor your progress

Just because you've plotted the course doesn't mean you can sit back and expect everything to happen for you. You need to remain engaged and thoughtful, constantly reviewing your progress. Course corrections may be needed at certain times—so pay attention!

To make sure you stay on track, keep your lists somewhere conspicuous. You won't forget your goals if they're in your face all the time. For instance:

- Use Outlook or another calendar program to set reminders and due dates for each goal.

- Post your one-year list on the fridge, then check off each item as the year progresses.

- Type up the list, shrink it, and stick it onto a business card. Carry this around in your wallet and pull it out to reflect on it occasionally.

Step 9: Watch for slippage

Because no plan is 100 percent successful as originally formulated, it's important for you to realize that your journey will not be one of continuous improvement each and every day. There will be the occasional misstep or setback. Recognize this and then be prepared for it when it happens.

Great performers in any business, sport, or other endeavor recognize that they will have setbacks and lessons to learn as they make their way to the top of their field. They accept this as a part of becoming the best possible. On the other side of the equation are those who believe that they are entitled to certain successes because they've worked hard to get them. When life hands them a setback, they are often the first to throw up their hands, saying that they tried, but that it's just not possible to get what they wanted.

It's called *game versus significance* in some fields of study. If you treat your journey as a game in which you will occasionally lose or miss, but you believe that you will indeed win in the end, it will happen—just as you expect. Don't allow yourself to start thinking that a slip backward or missed opportunity will prevent you from achieving your ultimate goal.

With an expectation that there are going to be occasional slides backward, and with the realization that setbacks are all just part of the game, you will surely get what you want out of this life.

In closing …

If you've made it this far, congratulations again! I realize that I am asking you to take a really hard look at what you are doing and assess how it meshes with what you want to do and be. It's not easy and many don't get this far.

I sincerely hope your personal action plan is exactly what you want for your life. If so, it will provide new balance, increased satisfaction, and success. I wish you great fortune as you roll out your plan over the coming days, months, and years.

John

The Author

Known as "the woman's success advocate," John McKee has been a business coach since 1988. A former senior executive who has worked in boardrooms and executive suites across North America, he was a part of the original founding senior executive team of DIRECTV prior to establishing BusinessSuccessCoach.net. He knows what works and what doesn't, and provides a wealth of information to his clients in a unique, easy-to-digest package.

John has created a new coaching method specifically for business clients. His **Four Windows Process** guides people through a series of steps in which they create a status review, then develop a game plan to move forward with clearly defined and clearly timelined objectives for career, finance, and personal life. Unlike other, more tactical coaching methods, the Four Windows Process is strategic, holistic, and encompassing. John's clients have found it to be an excellent tool for getting tangible results in a very short period of time.

What Are the Four Windows?

The Foundational Window	The Attributes Window
Reviewing your current life • What's great? • What's not as great? • What's not good? **Looking at a better future** • Your personal/family life • Your business/career • Your financial situation	**Assessing your strengths** • Recognizing and valuing your talents • Building on learned skills • Finding new opportunities **Understanding development areas** Awareness, not focus Being genuine The job environment
The Window of Evolvement	**The Window of Opportunity**
Developing the personal action plan • Set key goals • Reverse engineering • Replenishment options **Executing the action plan** • Set timelines • Identify action steps • Balance multiple targets	**Establish priorities** • Conjoint analysis • Intellectual vs. emotional choices • Action plan support **No walls will hold you back** • A life of ongoing success • The law of attraction • Anticipating slippage

More information is available at BusinessSuccessCoach.net.

CPSIA information can be obtained at www.ICGtesting.com
Printed in the USA
LVOW050314260712

291601LV00002B/37/A